DAY TRADING FUTURES:

Learn how Day Trading and Futures Work to Build your Financial Freedom. How to Become a Smart Trader to Don't Lose Money and Earn Passive Income with a Positive ROI in 19 Days

Alexander Taylor

© Copyright 2020 - All rights reserved.

The content contained within this book may not be reproduced, duplicated or transmitted without direct written permission from the author or the publisher.

Under no circumstances will any blame or legal responsibility be held against the publisher, or author, for any damages, reparation, or monetary loss due to the information contained within this book. Either directly or indirectly.

Legal Notice:

This book is copyright protected. This book is only for personal use. You cannot amend, distribute, sell, use, quote or paraphrase any part, or the content within this book, without the consent of the author or publisher.

Disclaimer Notice:

Please note the information contained within this document is for educational and entertainment purposes only. All effort has been executed to present accurate, up to date, and reliable, complete information. No warranties of any kind are declared or implied. Readers acknowledge that the author is not engaging in the rendering of legal, financial, medical or professional advice. The content within this book has been derived from various sources. Please consult a licensed professional before attempting any techniques outlined in this book.

By reading this document, the reader agrees that under no circumstances is the author responsible for any losses, direct or indirect, which are incurred as a result of the use of information contained within this document, including, but not limited to, errors, omissions, or inaccuracies.

TABLE OF CONTENTS

INTRODUCTION 8

CHAPTER 1: UNDERSTANDING DAY TRADING? 12
- How Day Trading Works 13
- Characteristics of a Day Trader 14
- Profit and Risks of Day Trading 17
- Short Trades and Long Trades 18
- Difference Between Day Trading and Swing Trading 19
- Retail vs. Institutional Traders 21
- Leverage 22
- High-Frequency Trading (HFT) 23

CHAPTER 2: FUTURES TRADING 24
- History of Future Trading 26
- Definition of a Futures Contract 26
- Why We Need Futures Markets 27
- How to Trade Futures 30
- Factors that Should Be Taken into Consideration 38
- Principles of Futures Trading 40
- Which Market to Trade and with Which Broker 41

CHAPTER 3: FUTURES SPREAD TRADING 46
- Futures Spreads Trading Pricing and Margins 49
- Market Types 50
- Common Spread Types: Commodity Futures 51

CHAPTER 4: HOW TO MAKE A PROFIT ON THE FUTURES MARKET 54
- When to Trade and When Not to Trade 54
- The Most Effective Method to Make Money Trading Futures 59
- Most Significant Hints on the Best Way to Profit in the Fates Advertise 61
- Exchanging Knowledge for Success in the Futures Market 63
- Tips for Intermediate Futures Options Traders 65
- Things That Distinguish Winning and Losing Traders in Options Trading ... 68

CHAPTER 5: GOLDEN TRADING RULES AND MISTAKES TO AVOID 72
- Trend Is Your Friend 72
- Always Plan Your Trade 72
- Protect Your Capital 73
- Don't Extend Losses 73
- Don't Be Greedy; Take a Timely Profit 73
- Leave Emotions Out of the Trading Ring 73

KEEP YOUR TRADING RECORD	73
DON'T LISTEN TO OTHERS	74
IF IN DOUBT, THEN DO NOT TRADE	74
OVERTRADING IS THE REAL ENEMY	74
HOLDING POSITIONS UNTIL THE SUBSEQUENT DAY IS RISK	74
CHOOSE A LIQUID MARKET TO TRADE	75
SETTLING OF CONTRACT	75
DON'T STAY ON THE TREND, FOLLOW IT	75
FOLLOW A SYSTEM, DON'T GET INTO CHAOS	75
ACCEPT LOSSES, ADJUST GAINS	76
HAVE A HEALTHY BUSINESS PLAN	76
THE IMPETUS FOR MERCANTILISM IS OUT	76
DISCIPLINE IS ESSENTIAL	76
VOLATILITY IS OFTEN EXPLOSIVE	77
FOLLOW AN IDEA, THINK ABOUT THE FUTURE	77
NOT TIMING THE MARKET CORRECTLY	77
MAKING INVESTMENTS THAT ARE TOO RISKY	77
MAKING INVESTMENTS THAT AREN'T RISKY ENOUGH	78
NOT KNOWING YOUR LIMITS	78
BEING OVERCONFIDENT	79
NEVER ONLY LOOK FOR INFORMATION THAT CONFIRMS WHAT YOU ALREADY BELIEVE	79
DON'T RESORT TO ANCHORING	79
ACCEPT THAT LOSS IS A PART OF THE PROCESS	80
PUTTING ALL YOUR EGGS IN ONE BASKET	80
INVESTING MORE THAN YOU CAN	81
GOING ALL IN BEFORE YOU'RE READY	81
FAILURE TO STUDY THE MARKETS	81
NOT GETTING ENOUGH TIME VALUE	81
NOT HAVING ADEQUATE LIQUIDITY	82
NOT HAVING A GRIP ON VOLATILITY	82
FAILING TO HAVE A PLAN	82
IGNORING EXPIRATION DATES	82
OVER-LEVERAGING	83
GIVING IN TO PANIC	83
CHAPTER 6: PROVEN AND TIME-TESTED FUTURES TRADING STRATEGIES	**84**
FUNDAMENTAL TRADING	84
TECHNICAL TRADING	84
COMPARING AND COMBINING MODELS	84
SUPPORT AND RESISTANCE	92
MOVING AVERAGES	93
TREND LINES	93

CHAPTER 7: TECHNICAL AND FUNDAMENTAL ANALYSIS 96
- TECHNICAL ANALYSIS 96
- FUNDAMENTAL ANALYSIS 105

CHAPTER 8: THE RIGHT RISK AND MONEY MANAGEMENT 118
- MANAGING YOUR MONEY 118
- IMPORTANT MONEY MANAGEMENT RULES FOR TRADERS 119
- MONEY MANAGEMENT SKILLS 123
- IMPORTANCE OF MONEY MANAGEMENT 125
- MANAGING YOUR MONEY 128
- HOW TO MANAGE RISK 130
- THE THREE-STEP RISK MANAGEMENT PLAN 136

CHAPTER 9: THE CORRECT TRADING PSYCHOLOGY 138
- WHY TRADING PSYCHOLOGY IS IMPORTANT 138
- PSYCHOLOGICALLY APPROACH TOWARD SUCCESS 141
- IMPLEMENTING AN ORGANIZED APPROACH 147

CONCLUSION 162

Introduction

Futures are financial agreements or contracts in which the parties involved agree to trade an asset at a future date with a fixed price. It can either be on buying an asset or selling of an asset at a future date and a fixed price as agreed by the trading parties. Futures are not subject to market or price fluctuations, irrespective of the market conditions or price of the asset on which the future has been agreed over; the trading parties must fulfill their obligation to sell the tradable asset or buy the tradable asset as at when due. It is made use of leverage, which requires the parties to deposit a percentage of the total price agreed on with a broker.

To invest in futures, you need the services of a broker whose role is to process access to the market for you. Choose only credible futures brokers to avoid getting dumped and abused. The various types of futures include commodity futures, currency futures, stock index futures, US Treasury futures, gold futures, etc.

The advantages of futures include speculation purposes, protection of price against price instability and market volatility, the compulsion of contract, and deposit of a percentage of the contract. Futures are used by investors for speculation purposes. For example, it is used by investors to speculate on the path or direction in which the price of a given asset or security is going to take.

Another advantage of futures is that prices are protected and secured. Futures lock down prices for the duration of its existence. It does not matter if the price of the underlying asset or commodity goes up, remains the same, and the price falls; the price that is set at the signing of the future remains. Individuals use it to protect themselves from possible price instability, while corporations use it to protect the prices of what they sell from violent and unfavorable price movements.

Futures are obligations binding on the parties that are signatories to it. Futures are a compulsory contract and cannot be dissolved until the terms of the futures are met. With futures, you can rest assured that the other party, even though it does not want to fulfill the terms of the contract any longer, will be forced by the legal implications.

Futures allow for a deposit of a percentage of the contract with a chosen broker. This payment is used to show and assure the other party of seriousness to go through with the terms and conditions of the futures.

Some of the disadvantages of futures include: it is not suitable for day trading, loss of margin, missing out on favorable price changes, and losses. Futures are not suitable for day trading as they have a future date in mind, which exceeds the trading window of a day trader. Futures are more suited to long term trading.

Futures make use of leverage, which means the trader is not obliged to deposit a hundred percent of the contract. In cases where the terms of the future do not favor the investor, the investor ends up losing his margin advantage.

Futures are useful when the price of the asset to be traded is favorable with the terms of the future. Investors can miss out on exciting and favorable price changes due to his or her obligation to the terms of the futures. It also applies to companies also involved in futures.

Futures have their prices fixed no matter the condition, rain, or sunshine. Futures can be a disadvantage to investors and corporations when instead of recording profit, the corporation or investor records losses caused by an unfavorable price movement. Futures are like a legendary two-edged sword; on one side, it can bless the investor or corporation with favorable price movements and result in bargain deals while, on the other hand, it can result in unfavorable price movements for the investor or corporation and result in losses and misses.

Futures contracts are a type of derivative in which the underlying asset of the contract is paid for in advance of its delivery. Futures deal almost exclusively in commodities though there may be futures contracts in other assets such as currency. Futures are generally traded on all major stock trades around the world. Therefore, futures are not just limited to one specific trade.

Since futures deal with assets whose price fluctuates according to market conditions, keeping open positions for a more extended period may expose investors to sudden market fluctuations. For instance, oil futures tend to be the riskiest of all.

Since day trading implies opening and closing positions on the same day, investors can avoid the ups and downs that come with leaving positions overnight. Besides, futures are often traded after the close of markets in the United States. That implies that fluctuations in Asian markets will have a direct impact on futures traded in the United States.

So, if oil futures fall during trading in Asia, an investor in North America may wake up to an unpleasant surprise. By cashing out at the end of the day, day traders can ensure there will be no surprises at the beginning of the next trading day.

Advanced day traders may choose to keep positions open overnight. However, derivatives are the riskiest type of investment vehicles. This is why investors need to be clear on the advantages and disadvantages that come with dabbling in these markets.

The trades facilitate trading between buyers and sellers. To trade futures, traders need to put up cash, which is commonly referred to as margin in futures trading. A proper margin must be maintained for the life of the trade. Traders need to have a sufficient margin to trade futures. This will usually depend on the kind of future that is being traded and how many contracts.

Chapter 1:
Understanding Day Trading?

Day trading is regularly associated with its traders exiting their positions before the market closes. The main aim of this act is to avoid risks that cannot be managed and price gaps that are negative. The negative price gaps can result from the closing one-day prices and opening of the following day prices at the open.

Day trading often involves the use of margin leverage. A good depiction of this phenomenon can be used in the United States of America. Regulation T has the potential to permit initial maximum leverage of up to 2:1. However, many brokers go to levels of promoting up to 4:1 leverage during the moments the leverages are reduced to 2:1 or even less. This is mostly done near the end of the trading day.

The market of United States terms traders who trade for more than four days as pattern day traders. These forms of traders have an obligation to maintain a minimum of twenty-five thousand dollars in their accounts as equity.

Traders in the day can end up not fees for interests that are charged for margin benefit. It is because margin interest is a typical charge for the balances that are accrued at midnight. However, this does not brush away the risks of a margin call that are experienced sometimes.

A broker is a person who is the determinant of the margin interests because of his or her call. There are several financial instruments that are commonly traded in the modern era day trading. These financial instruments include currencies, stocks, contracts for difference, hosts for future contracts, and options. The common future contracts that are traded include interest rates futures, commodity futures, and equity index futures.

There was a time day trading was an exclusive activity. It was a form of trade that was associated with professional speculators and financial firms. A large portion of day trading individuals are the employees of banks and other financial institutions. This group of employees tasked with such roles is always good specialists in managing funds and equity investment.

The year 1975 saw the popularization of day trading with several parties joining the trade. It was because the commissions in the United States were deregulated. The rise of electronic platforms for trading was witnessed in the years of 1990s. The volatility of stock prices was also seen during the periods of the dot-com bubble, as represented in Figure 1 below. Scalping is a new intraday trading technique that is used by traders in the day trading. It involves holding the trading position for a couple of minutes or seconds.

Day trading is basically the purchasing and selling of securities within a single trading day in any marketplace at commonly stock markets and foreign exchange (FOREX) for the purpose of obtaining a compound of short-term loans.

How Day Trading Works

Day trading is a career that you have to invest time into. If you have decided to try it out, you have to spend time practicing it before you start live trading. As you practice, you improve your strategies. Only then do you use live money to try it out? All these need you to invest your time. Day trading isn't something that can be done successfully only when you have the urge for it. You must spend your time and energy on it if you want to succeed.

If you have decided that trading is something that you want to consider, you should think of starting up as little as possible. Go for a few stocks or currencies initially, instead of trying to enter the market with a boom, and at the end of the day, you thin yourself out. If you go all out initially, you will end up confusing yourself, and this could lead to a large number of losses. It is advisable that you are calm while you trade. Shut off your emotions while you trade. Use only facts and don't try to make use of emotions because they could mislead you.

The more you are able to take out the emotional aspect, the more you can be true to the plan that you have laid out. When you are calm, it permits you to be focused.

Characteristics of a Day Trader

Being a day trader does come out naturally; a specific personality and traits are duly required. Below are some of the characteristics of a day trader.

Disciplined

This is a major trait that day traders really need to input. Day traders should always be disciplined to remain input when no opportunities emerge and really act so fast when opportunities avail. Acting fast also includes strictly considering the step by step rules and obligations initially formed in their big plans.

Open-minded

Day trading is a learning kind of income-generating engagement, implying that there are going to be happy times and downfalls. Save yourself and learn from all that. Improve the happy times and completely discard the downfall of wrong moves. Being exposed to the winnings and the failures makes you open-minded, master of all possible win moves.

A Fan of Technology

Day trading is carried out in various trading platforms and systems that a trader should be familiarized with. This should not scare you. Getting to know how they work does not, in any case, require you to be a computer whiz. Get to learn the basic moves and grow technologically with time.

Mentally Tough

Losing market trades are constant; most successful traders will have losing trades every single day. They typically win slightly more times than they lose. It is so important to stay focused and rational during a losing period and do not let in the basic fact that money has been lost too. Focus on the future day trading activities by implementing some of the strategies outlined in a big plan.

Independence

Independence is striving to build your own toolbox that is, and willy forever lead you. Reading trading books to trading books, watching each and every video, interacting with one mentor after the other, can be a total miss. What if different books have one confusing point on a particular field? What is your YouTube subscriber who decides to quit vlogging? Always grasp the basics after in-depth research and day stay put. Dare to yourself that you got you and get the large chunks of benefits. However, when you feel you are so lost, do not hesitate to get assistance. Most importantly, master and analyze successful moves and let them be part of your big plan.

Patience

Good things do take quite some time. In every strategical move you try to make, think about it carefully, but this should not make you paranoid. Act accordingly with many disciplines to reduce the number of losses likely to be incurred during various day trading activities.

Also, a patient day trader is a learning day trader. Day trading is not going to be easy at first, but with time, where you will be equipped with lots of skills and experience, things are expected to flow very smoothly. Hey, be patient.

Future-oriented

Getting stuck in the past makes you much of a prisoner. Forward-thinking lets you see the possible moves and gives you the decisive air when the next trading activity will occur considering the set protocols set in the day trader's plan. Being future-oriented incites forward-thinking, which is basically clearly involves mental thinking and knowing your next possible moves after a considerate examination. Being future-oriented hastens and simplifies the day trading operation moves, and the chances are that they are going to be successful.

Financial freedom

Day trading does not require you to be a tycoon necessarily, but you are required to have a specific amount of money that has been precisely selected to begin day trading with. Remember, the first times are always a win or lose situation as you continue to learn and grow. This particular set of money can be lost too. Be careful about how you handle your finances in day trading. Not every story is a good story.

Enthusiasm

A great interest in something is a pending successful goal. A great enthusiastic inclination to stocks, securities, commodities, markets, the business gives you the thirst to learn and master what day trading is all about. These are signs of a future successful day trader.

Experience and Familiarity

Experience comes with pretty much of downfall lessons and learning. Expose yourself to different learning sources and master every profitable move during day trading so as to squeeze the best out of that. Getting the actual experience and familiarity of the trading platforms and various strategies needed to be successful at day trading is worthwhile.

Profit and Risks of Day Trading

The process of day trading involves sloppy financial leverage, and speedy returns are probable. This phenomenon makes the trade to either be extremely profitable or extremely unprofitable. Those people who are described as high-risk profile traders are also greatly impacted by such a phenomenon.

These groups of traders have the probability of making enormous percentages of profit or, on the other hand, undergo massive amounts of parentage loss. Day trading trader's individuals are sometimes referred to as bandits or gamblers by other traders or investors. It is because these traders can either make huge amounts of profits or losses during the trade. There are several factors that can make this form of trade to be very risky while an individual is trading. They include individual trading on trade with low odds instead of trading on a trade that has high odds of winning; the presence of risk capital that is inadequate, which is tied together with overload stress of surviving and presence of poor management of funds which entails poor execution of the trade.

Gains and losses are mostly amplified by the popular usage of buying on margin. The process of buying on margin can be described as the use of borrowed funds. This action usually results in a trader experiencing a substantial loss or gain in a short span during the day. Brokers have the common tendency of allowing bigger trade margins for day traders.

Short Trades and Long Trades

The terms regarding short trades are common terms to an individual who is participating in stock trading. These terms are majorly used in situations where a trader is either buying or selling first. There are several expectations that a trader always has in mind if he or she is either doing short trade or long trade.

When a trader is participating in a short trade, he or she purchases the financial instruments with the aim of selling them at a higher price in the future to make profits. On the other hand, short trade involves a trader selling financial instruments with the intent of later buying them at a lower price so as to make his or her profits.

Long Trade

Some day traders are common participants in the long trade. They are purchase financial instruments with hopes that they will increase in value. This makes their prices to increase in turn. The term that is mostly used by day traders always buys and long, which are interchangeable. Software developed to help long trade, with buttons that are either marked long or buy. These buttons are used to represent an open position entered by a trader. This position simply means an individual has shares in a certain firm or trade. When a trader decides to go long, he or she is always interested in purchasing a certain financial instrument. If the decision for such is perused, the potential for profit levels is always unlimited. It is because the prices of the purchased financial instruments can get higher indefinitely.

This is despite a day trader participating in small moves. The risks in this form of trade have a lower risk potential of the purchased instruments to fall to zero. It is because profits and risks are always controlled by the multiple small moves that are made.

Short Trade

Day traders in short trades always sell their financial instruments before purchasing them. During moments they buy the financial instrument, they hope the prices will have gone down. This the moment they are able to realize their profits because they will be buying the financial instruments at a lower price from that which they had sold.

Short trading is one of the most confusing forms of trade because people across the globe are used to buying first before selling. However, one can sell and buy in the financial markets.

There are common terms that are used by traders participating in short trades. These terms include short and sell, which are used interchangeably. Software developed to aid short trade also has buttons marked short or sell. The term short usually means a trader has an open position to shorting some financial instruments.

Profit levels are always limited in this situation when compared to the initial amount that was used to purchase the financial instruments. Various traders are used to taking short positions to reduce or minimize risks.

Difference Between Day Trading and Swing Trading

The main aim of traders in business is to be able to generate profit. There are several forms of trading that can be used. For an individual to understand what day trading is about, he or she is supposed to also have insight about swing trading. Having this knowledge and knowing the difference between swing trade and day trade will help them have a clear line of how to perform the trade to impeccable standards.

The first step to understanding swing trading is by getting what its definition is. This is the form of trade that involves a trader to buy or sell financial instruments and hold them for a varied time of a few days. The holding on time of financial instruments can go on to an extended period of several weeks.

There are several factors that can make a trader practicing swing trade to be in a sell or buy position. These circumstances are based on technical, quantitative, or fundamental valuations by the trader. Such occurrence may mean that a swing trader may take longer working periods than the day trader.

Most people who practice swing trade have a common set of beliefs amongst themselves. They mostly go for the thought of accumulating gains or losses. This process is done in a swift manner that is very slow and smooth compared to day trading.

However, there are certain instances where a trader practicing swing trading can experience swings in his or her trades. The results of these swings are always too extreme in two ways. He or she can either gain large percentages of profits or experience huge percentages of loss in a very short time. Individual trading as a swing trader usually does not take part as a full-time trader in the market.

There are four key differences between swing trading and day trading. They include:

An individual practicing day trading sells or buys financial instruments and liquidates his or her position on the same day. On the other hand, a swing trader upholds his or her position for a variation of days or even weeks. A person in day trading is meant to invest a huge number of hours in a day so as to be able to monitor the flow of prices in their portfolios. However, a swing trader is estimated to use few hours in trading as he or she can maintain his or her position for days or weeks.

Day trading is involved with several sessions of being fast-paced and having adrenaline rushes. It is because there are quick decisions to be made, and the trade is fast-paced. This is the exact opposite of people who practice swing trading. It is they are required to be calm when making decisions because they focus more on the long-term return.

Day trading involves the usage of an advanced system of charting. The charting system is designed to accommodate short intervals of trade. These intervals can be programmed to track one to up to thirty minutes. However, swing traders are prone to using a less complex charting system. These charting systems can be programmed to monitor the market for a varied time of about one to four or five hours.

Retail vs. Institutional Traders

In the world of trading, there are basically two forms of traders: institutional and retail. The difference between them dictates the way they approach their trades. For example, institutional traders usually make large trades as compared to retail traders. But what are they exactly?

Their names might just give you a clue as to what you can understand about them.

The term "Retail traders" refers to individual traders. These traders can be anyone in the world who has the ability to get in on a trade. On the other hand, institutional traders are those who represent large financial institutions, hedge funds, banks, or other big firms that manage money. You could say that institutional traders are "corporate" traders, whereas retail traders are "home" traders.

So, does the amount invested in the trade dictate the type of trader one becomes? Is that the only point of distinction?

Not quite.

Analysis

A retail trader usually prefers to use some sort of technical analysis system for their trades. They utilize price patterns and behaviors in the past or indicators in the present that dictate future price scenarios. On the other hand, institutional traders do not usually refer to only technical patterns or systems to show them opportunities in their trade.

Focus

As institutional traders have been dealing with the system for a long time, their experience has led them to hone their skills well. They make use of market sentiments and fundamentals. They make use of trading psychology (which is a firm grasp on their emotions and keeping an analytical mind despite the situation) and understanding of overall responses towards a currency. They are keeping a close eye on the news to see if there are certain trends or reactions that they can pick up on.

Retail traders are not experienced in managing risks or having a proper psychological mind for trading. However, this is a situation that happens to everyone who gets started in Forex trading. No one can be prepared for what they will experience. They have to experience it first before they can decide how to keep their minds sharp.

Leverage

Institutional traders do not usually use leverage. Their main attention is spent on risk management. Even if a situation were to occur where they had to make use of leverages, they would be careful about how much leverage they are going to use.

On the other hand, retail traders make the mistake of looking for brokers that provide them with high leverages. While that act in itself is not wrong, it does pose a problem to those retailers who choose their brokers solely on the criteria of how much leverage those brokers provide them.

Now that we have understood more about the Forex market and its players, it is time we look at the most essential component of the market, currencies. More importantly, we are going to look at some of the major players in the Forex market.

High-Frequency Trading (HFT)

This trading technique entails high-frequency trades. It is perhaps the riskiest, most complex, and involved style of trading, which demands speed and attention on a 24-hour basis. Traders using this technique rely on analyzing multiple markets concurrently for profits. Successful traders in this segment are able to evaluate their composite and trademarked systems of trading. Usually, a beginner, perhaps working from home, is usually not competitive in this market. This trading approach differs from day trading since day trading follows a one market approach.

Essentially, day trading differs from all these trading mechanisms because of the holding period of the stocks bought. Remember that trading mainly entails buying low and selling high. Also, remember that day trading entails entering and exiting the market within the same day. Day trading is often like a full-time job, where you have to identify and ensure that all requisites are in order. Any disruptions of the working space can make traders miss the intraday price fluctuations and hence miss their best trading opportunities. However, it is not as complex, intensive, or risky as scalp trading, which takes less trading spans and stricter conditions.

Chapter 2:
Futures Trading

What happens when you buy futures is one of the most frequent questions about futures trading. When you buy futures, you are accepting to purchase products or service the company from which you bought futures has not produced yet. In comparison to stock trading, futures trading is much riskier because you deal with products and services that are not yet produced. With such characteristics, future trading is very popular among the producing companies and individuals and customers and speculators.

While stocks or shares are being traded on stock markets, futures are being traded on futures markets. The idea of future markets developed from the needs of agricultural producers in the mid-nineteenth century, where often happened that the demand was much bigger than supply.

The difference between the futures markets and futures markets today is that today's futures markets have crossed the borders of agricultural production and entered many other sectors, such as financial. As such, future markets today are used to buy and sell currencies and other financial instruments.

What future markets made possible is the opportunity for a farmer to participate in the goods with customers on the other end of the world. One of the biggest and most important future markets is the International Monetary Market (IMM), established in 1972.

Futures are financial derivatives that obtain their value from the movement in the price of another asset. It means that the futures price is not dependent on its inherent value. Still, on the amount of the asset, the futures contract is tracking.

One of the advantages of the futures market is that it is centralized and that people from around the world electronically can make future contracts. These future contracts will specify the price of the merchandise and the time of delivery. Every future contract contains information about the quality and the quantity of the sold goods, specific prices, and the method in which the goods are to be delivered to the buyers.

A person who buys or sells a futures contract does not pay for the whole value of the contract. He pays a small upfront fee to trigger an open position. For example, if the futures contract's value is $350,000 when the S&P 500 is 1400, he only pays $21,875 as its initial margin. The exchange sets this margin and may change anytime.

If the S&P 500 moved up to 1500, the futures contract would be worth $375,000. Thus, the person will earn $25,000 in profit.

However, if the index fell to 1390 from its original 1400, he will lose $2,500 because the futures contract will now be worth $347,500. This $2,500 is not a realized loss yet. The broker will also not require the individual to add more cash to his trading account.

However, if the index fell to 1300, the futures contract will be worth $325,000. The individual loses $50,000. The broker will require him to add more money to his trading account because his initial margin of $21,875 is no longer enough to cover his losses.

History of Future Trading

The history of futures trading began on the Midwestern frontier of the United States of America in the early 1800s. Chicago's strategic location, at the base of the Great Lakes and close to the Midwest's fertile farmlands, contributed to the city's rapid growth and development as a grain terminal.

In 1848, 82 merchants formed a central marketplace, the Chicago Board of Trade. Their purpose was to promote commerce in the city by providing a place where buyers and sellers could meet to exchange commodities. Growing use of contracts that specified delivery of a particular commodity at a predetermined price and date made the CBOT increasingly popular as a central marketplace.

These early forward contracts in corn were first used by river merchants. They received farmers' corn in late autumn and early winter and needed to ship it to grain producers such as flour mills, bread manufacturers, etc. Often the corn needed to be stored all winter.

Definition of a Futures Contract

The best futures contracts you will find in the market.

S&P 500 E-mini

Most traders will fancy the idea of trading in the S&P 500 E-mini because of its high liquidity aspect. It also appeals to most investors because of its low day trading margins. You can conveniently trade in S&P 500 E-mini around the clock, not to mention that you will also benefit from its technical analysis aspect. Essentially, the S&P 500 E-mini is a friendly contract since you can easily predict its price patterns.

10 Year T-Notes

10 Year T-Notes is also ranked as one of the best contracts to trade in. Considering its sweet maturity aspect, most traders would not hesitate to trade in this futures contract. There are low margin requirements that a trader will have to meet when trading in 10 Year T-Notes.

Crude Oil

Crude oil also stands as one of the most popular commodities in futures trading. It is an exciting market because of its high daily trading volume of about 800k. Its high volatility also makes the market highly lucrative.

Gold

This is yet another notable futures contract. It might be expensive to trade in gold; however, it is a great hedging choice, more so in poor market conditions.

Why We Need Futures Markets

Let's take a simple example. A farmer is planting his crop and wants to be certain he will obtain a particular price for his crop of corn. He feels comfortable with the current corn price and wants to protect himself from a falling price. Suppose he wants to be able to obtain $4 per bushel for his crop, which is due for harvesting and delivery in October, regardless of what happens to the market price. The market price can fluctuate as a result of weather conditions or supply and demand between now and harvesting time in October. One corn contract consists of 5,000 bushels, so he sells a sufficient number of contracts to cover his entire October crop at $4 a bushel through his broker on a commodity exchange like the Chicago Board of Trade.

After a spell of good weather, the predicted bumper crop materializes in October, and because of this, the cash price for one bushel of corn drops to $3.

The farmer is not concerned because he has guaranteed himself a price of $4, so he buys contracts at $3, which offsets against the contracts he sold for $4, giving himself a profit of $1 dollar per bushel. This profit offsets the loss on the cash price when the crop is harvested, and he ends up with $4 per bushel.

This is known as hedging.

Conversely, a bread manufacturer will use this technique to protect him from rising prices. The manufacturer will buy enough October contracts at $4 as a hedge against rising prices. If the price jumps to $6 per bushel because of floods or drought, he will profit from the increased value of his contracts, offsetting the increased cash price he has to pay for wheat.

Where Do We Fit in?

There are many people like you and me who trade simply to make money. Some are big institutional investors, but the majority of the market consists of small investors or speculators.

All of the speculators, large or small, provide a vital function to the futures market by buying or selling millions of contracts every day, and by doing so, provide liquidity to the markets.

 Without liquidity, the markets cannot function.

Futures Market Categories

There are similarities in all futures contracts. However, each contract may track different assets

As such, it is essential to study the various markets that exist.

Categories of Futures Markets				
Agriculture	Grains	Livestock	Dairy	Forest
Energy	Crude Oil	Heating oil	Natural gas	Coal
Stock Index	S&P 500	Nasdaq 100	Nikkei 225	E-mini S&P 500
Foreign Currency	Euro/USD	GBP/USD	Yen/USD	Euro/Yen
Interest Rates	Treasuries	Money markets	Interest Rate Swaps	Barclays Aggregate Index
Metals	Gold	Silver	Platinum	Base Metals

You can trade futures contracts on different categories and assets. However, if you are still a new trader, it is important to trade assets that you know. For example, if you are into stock trading for a few years already, you must start with futures contracts using stock indexes. This way, you won't have a hard time understanding the underlying asset. You only need to understand how the futures market works.

After choosing a category, decide on the asset that you want to trade. For example, you want to trade futures contracts in the energy category. Focus on coal, natural gas, crude oil, or heating oil. The markets trade at various levels, so you must understand relevant things, likes the nuances, liquidity, margin requirements, contract sizes, and volatility. Do the necessary research before trading in futures contracts.

How to Trade Futures

The safest way to trade a futures contract is with Stop-Loss orders. They are just what they sound like—instructions to staunch the bleeding at a predetermined level. They can also be used to lock in profits, so Stop-Loss orders are good to have in an investor's toolbox.

Stop-Loss orders are placed at the same time a trade is entered. For instance, take Frozen concentrated orange juice contracts, Dan Aykroyd was waving around for sale at $1.42. The price would eventually fall to 29 cents. That would spell ruin for anyone buying those contracts, as it did for Ralph Bellamy and Don Ameche. But if they had bought Aykroyd's contract with a stop-order of $1.40, they would have parachuted out of the position automatically when the price fell below $1.40, saving most of their fortune.

On the other hand, if the price rose to $1.50, Bellamy and Ameche could move their original stop-order from $1.40 to $1.48 and ensure they would profit by at least eight cents should the price of frozen concentrated orange juice begin falling back down.

Of course, safety in investing often comes with a price tag. Using the example of a stop-order at $1.40, let's say that the price dropped briefly to $1.38 and then shot quickly up over $1.50. Those profits will not be padding your bank account because you are automatically moved out of the contract as soon as the price hits your Stop-Loss order limit.

Never cancel a Stop-Loss order once you place it. You initiated the order—hopefully—as part of a sound investment strategy, and you do not want to bid it farewell due to an emotional reaction to later events. And never change your position in a market without sound, rational motives. If you are the type who likes to work without a net, you can avoid using Stop-Loss orders but always realize that you can lose significantly more money trading futures than may sit in your account.

The reason a Stop-Loss order is critical is the margin call. Since you are investing only a small percentage of the value of the contract, you must maintain a minimum amount of money in your account, called the maintenance margin. If the price of the commodity tumbles below that level, a margin call is issued for you to bring the amount of your account back up to its initial level. If a margin call is issued, you must pay up immediately, or the brokerage has to right to liquidate your entire position to cover the losses. That is why people were jumping off buildings when the stock market crashed in 1929.

As with your entire investment portfolio, diversity can be the key to minimizing risk in trading futures. The best traders in the world limit their position in a single commodity to between 3 and 5% of their trading capital. You should certainly do the same. Build positions in as broad a selection of markets as you feel you have knowledge. That may include positions in corn, gold, crude oil, and the Nasdaq, for instance. But never enter a market without judgment to support your move—do not try to build a diversified futures portfolio for diversity's sake.

When searching for new markets to flesh out a portfolio, look beyond the big exchanges like the Chicago Board of Trade or the Chicago Mercantile Exchange and investigate other exchanges where you can take on much smaller contracts—as much as 80% smaller. This way, you can ease your way into the vagaries of commodities. You can also engage in paper trading (using make-believe trades and following real-market results for a period of time) if you find that way of learning about new investments helpful, but it is never like trading with real money.

Find a Good Broker

One of the critical decisions that you will make when you first get started in trading is who you will hire as your broker. There are many brokers out there, so this can be a hard decision to choose who will be the right one.

The first thing to determine is how much time you plan to put into your investing and how much help you will need. Some people like to do the work all on their own, and others will need some hand-holding to get them started at least. There are brokers out there that can help with both situations; you just need to know what your situation is before you start looking.

Then, you need to take a look at some of the fees that the broker is going to charge. If the fees are too high, then they will start to eat into your profits, and that is never a good thing. All brokers are going to charge you some fees to invest and use them, so that is something you should expect right from the beginning. However, the way they charge these fees and the amount that you spend on these fees over time is going to depend on each broker.

Decide How Much You Can Spend

This is a tricky one to work with because the amount will depend on your budget. Any amount can be used to make trading profitable. You have to keep in mind never to trade more than you can afford to lose.

One way to make sure that you follow this rule is to set up a separate account that you would like to use just for trading money. Each month, add in the amount that you can safely invest without hurting your other finances, and that is all that you can trade on. That way, if you make a few bad trades, you have not lost all of the money that you need for making the house payment or something else that needs to be paid that month.

Choosing to Buy Long or Sell Short

The price of a stock is going to do one of three things at a given time. It will go down, go up, or it will move sideways. When you enter into the market as a swing trader, you are expecting that the stock is going to go up, or it will go down. If you think that the stock will see an increase in its price, then they will purchase the stock. This move is going to be considered "going long" or having a "long position" in that stock. For example, if you are long 100 shares of Facebook Inc., it means that you purchased 100 shares of this company, and you are making the prediction that you will be able to sell them at a higher price later on and earn a nice profit.

How to Enter a Trade

If you are brand new to trading, you are probably curious about how you would sell or purchase security. Any time that the market is open, there are going to be two prices for any security that can be traded. There will be the bid price and the ask price. The bid price is what buying or purchasing traders are offering to pay for that stock right then. The ask price, on the other hand, is the price that traders want in order to sell that security.

You will quickly notice that the bid price is always going to be a bit lower simply because the buyers want to pay less, and the asking price is always going to be higher because sellers want more for their holdings. The difference between these two prices is known as the spread.

The spreads that are found will vary for each stock, and they can even change throughout the day. If a stock doesn't have a ton of buyers and sellers, then there could be a bigger spread. When there are more buyers and sellers, then the spread between these two prices will be much lower.

Investment and Margin Accounts

There are two types of accounts that you can choose to open in order to trade stocks. The two main options include the margin account and the investment account. With a margin account, you can borrow against the capital that you have placed in your account. The investment account, on the other hand, will allow you to buy up to the dollar value you hold in that account. You are not able to spend more than what you have put in that account at a time.

When you decide to open up a margin account, you may be able to borrow money from the investment or brokerage firm to help pay for some of your investment. This is a process that is known as buying on margin. This can provide you with some advantages of purchasing more shares that you would be able to afford if you just used the capital in your account, and it can help you leverage to get more profits with your money.

However, there is a catch with this one in the form of more risks. When you borrow the money to make your investments, there will come a point when you must pay the loan back. If you earn the profits that you think you will, it is easy to pay this back. But, if you lose out and make the wrong predictions, you are going to have to find other ways to pay the money back. Making investments with leverage can magnify the percentage losses on your money.

As a beginner, you should stick with a regular investment account. Trading on margin can increase the amount of risk that you are taking on in your trades. This may be tempting because it can increase your potential profits, but there is a lot more risk that comes with it as well. You will do much better going with an investment account instead. This way, you can just pull out the money that you are comfortable with rather than hoping that you make a good prediction in the beginning when you are learning.

Picking out How Much You Want to Invest

Finally, before we move into talking about some of the different swing trading platforms that you can work with, we need to discuss some of the basics of how much you are going to invest in your account. Since we have already discussed the importance of working with an investment account rather than trying to do the trading on margin, you will need to decide how much money you would like to put into your account. First, talk with your brokerage firm and decide how much you need to put in to meet their requirements. Some brokerage firms will ask you to spend a certain amount or keep a certain amount in your accounts at all times in order to trade. If your chosen firm has that kind of requirement, then make sure that you put in at least that much. Putting in more is up to your discretion.

Do Some Research

Research is your best friend when you go through this process. The more time you can spend researching and look at charts, the more you will understand how the market works and how much you can make on it in the process.

There are a few other resources that you can spend your time on to make sure that you see the best results and that you can take your trading to the next level. Sources from the news are an excellent place to start because they can provide you with some great information that the company is releasing or what other analysts are saying as well.

Know What Good Futures Contracts Look Like

You should be aware of what a good futures contract is. Before commencing any trade, you should obtain as much information as possible to make sure that you do not come across any unexpected situations. A significant point to note is that there may be several significant differences between futures contracts that need to be taken into account before moving ahead. You should be aware of the particular contract unit because each prospective futures contract will depict the size and the units it is trading in. A specific currency will always be used to denote forex futures, whereas those that depend on stock indices usually consist of a reference point on the index multiplied by a given price per share. The details of this measurement are generally not very significant as they are only critical at the moment to enable you to comprehend precisely what you are becoming involved in.

Choosing Right Contract

You should ensure that you choose the correct contract. Before selecting the appropriate agreements, you should comprehend the different degrees of insecurity that are occurring within the market in comparison to the possibility of a severe payout in case everything works out well. This is important because there is a significantly higher variance in the futures market compared to other markets because they include a much higher variety. When such kinds of decisions are to be made, a significant point to note is that in this case, the previous results are not going to forecast future outcomes accurately. This indicates that even though the price has stayed constant for many days, it does not need to remain so in the future.

Look for the Right Signals

You need to determine the correct signals. When carrying out day trading of futures, you should remember that you will be able to achieve the best outcomes when you use three indicators that do not particularly have a link with each other. You should observe the sine wave as a way of identifying the price concerning resistance and support, the momentum to determine the volume in comparison to the supply, and the pro-am to identify the particular trade size, which will help you find out the degree to which the market is interested in the trade at that point.

Factors that Should Be Taken into Consideration

Before you go into an exchange, there are a few key factors that you should take a gander at other than the pattern and exchange arrangements, and they are:

Margins

When you enter into a trade, the exchanges will require a margin to be paid as your insurance that you will fulfill the terms of the contract. The size of margins can differ substantially from one commodity contract to the next. For example, an index contract margin like the S&P 500 can be as high as $25,000, whereas some of the grain contracts can be as low as $400. The amount of margin depends on the size of the contract and the volatility of the commodity. Make sure that you have enough money in your trading account to cover your margin. If your contract position makes a profit, you will get back your margin plus your profit. If your contract position is making a loss and the loss exceeds the size of your trading account, you will get a call from your broker requesting you to replenish your account with more funds immediately to maintain your trading position. This is called a margin call.

Volume

Before you enter into a trade, it is essential to check the volume of the contract. Volume is the number of contracts traded daily. To calculate the volume of a particular day, you have to add only the number of long contracts for that day and not the short contracts. Remember, the futures market is called a net sum zero game. In other words, for every winning trade, you have a losing trade, and with every trade, you have someone buying and someone selling a contract. Markets with a high volume give you the chance to enter and exit a trade at the levels of your choice. If the volume is too low, no one may be able to take the other side of your trade. This means that you are likely to get poor execution on your orders.

Capital Requirements

The amount of money required to begin trading in futures will vary. Some brokers will require a trader to have about $5,000. However, there are those who would require only $2,000. It is vital for a trader to choose the best broker who is flexible enough to allow them to trade with the little capital they have.

Leverage

Leverage will also vary depending on the type of futures you trade in. The contract value will also have an impact on the amount of leverage that you will have.

Liquidity

Just like leverage, the liquidity aspects of futures will also depend on the futures you are trading. Accordingly, it is important for any trader to regularly check the respective volumes of contracts before trading on them.

Volatility

Futures are volatile. The advantage gained by using high leverage ensures that a trader makes a good profit with little price changes in the market.

Keeping the above factors into consideration, futures are a good market to trade. A trader can easily day trade with as little as $2,000. The high leverage ratio will also guarantee that huge profits can be earned.

Open Interest

This is the number of contracts still open at the end of each day. It is also a useful guide for the market's liquidity. Low open interest indicates little trading interest, and potentially bad "fills" are very likely.

Principles of Futures Trading

"What actually happens when you buy futures?" It is actually one of the most frequent questions in relation to futures trading. The answer to this question can be summarized in a sentence that states: when you buy futures, you are actually accepting to buy products or services that the company from which you bought futures has not produced yet.

In comparison to stock trading, futures trading is much riskier because you deal with products and services that are not yet produced. With such characteristics, future trading is very popular not only among the producing companies and individuals and customers but also among speculators as well.

While stocks or shares are being traded on stock markets, futures are being traded on futures markets. The idea of future markets developed from the needs of agricultural producers in the mid-nineteenth century, where often happened that the demand was much bigger than supply.

The difference between the futures markets and futures markets today is that today's futures markets have crossed the borders of agricultural production and entered many other sectors, such as financial. As such, future markets today are used for buying and selling currencies as well as some other financial instruments. What future markets made possible is the opportunity for a farmer to be able to participate in the goods with customers on the other end of the world. One of the biggest and most important future markets is the International Monetary Market (IMM) that was established in 1972.

Futures are financial derivatives that obtain their value from the movement in the price of another asset. It means that the price of futures is not dependent on its inherent value but on the price of the asset the futures contract is tracking.

One of the advantages of the futures market is that it is centralized and that people from around the world electronically are able to make future contracts. These futures contracts will specify the price of the merchandise and the time of delivery. Besides that, every future contract contains information about the quality and the quantity of the sold goods, specific prices, and the method in which the goods are to be delivered to the buyers. A person who buys or sells a futures contract does not pay for the whole value of the contract. He pays a small upfront fee to trigger an open position. For example, if the value of the futures contract is $350,000 when the S&P 500 is 1400, he only pays $21,875 as its initial margin. The exchange sets this margin and may change anytime.

Which Market to Trade and with Which Broker

There is a huge array of products to trade with on offer, but for scalping, you need products with large volumes exchanged and volatility. I find these in the mini DAX and the e-mini Dow futures. The volatility, i.e., daily range (distance between the low of the day and the high of the day), is wide. In addition, and this point is very important, these products are traded on regulated and centralized markets: Eurex for the DAX futures and CME for the e-mini Dow, as opposed to CFDs, which are OTC products; i.e., your broker is the counterpart of your trade. When you buy, your broker is your seller, and when you sell, your broker is buying from you. On the other hand, on a centralized market, your order is routed and executed when someone else's order matches yours (buyers' and sellers' prices meet). In addition, on the futures markets, you can see the volume of transactions, while on the CFD, your broker may show no volume at all or only the volumes exchanged on their platform.

And more importantly, on the futures markets, you see the prices offered by other market participants, while on CFDs, you only get the prices offered by your broker. To illustrate, this I have just taken below a snapshot of prices offered by two different CFD brokers at the same time.

Which Broker Offers the Right Price?

In case of high volatility, CFDs do not react the same way as futures: the prices may adjust at a different pace, and the spread offered by the broker may increase. A market order may even be repriced if the market is moving very quickly. Stop orders may incur slippage, which means you will lose a few points to your broker as the price you are paid is a few points away from your stop order.

So, I can only recommend that you trade with future or mini futures contracts. However, CFDs can be useful to trade small positions when you make your first steps in trading as you can trade products at only one euro per point instead of 5 euros on a mini futures contract or even 25 euros per point on the DAX future. Note that CFDs are not available in all countries due to local laws and financial regulations.

But if you can and want to trade CFDs, make sure you look at the spreads offered by different brokers before choosing who to trade with. Half a point is not much different, but in scalping, it means a lot. After 20 trades, paying half a point more on each trade at one euro per point will result in an extra 10 euros wasted in commissions; and so on, after 40 trades, you will have wasted 20 euros. Let's say in a month if you perform 600 to 800 trades; you will then have wasted 300 to 400 euros in extra commissions.

How to Choose Your Broker

In order to be able to scalp in good conditions, you need to look out for the following points when choosing your broker:

Tight spreads if you choose to work with CFDs. One euro or dollar per point is the maximum you should pay as you don't want to be working just for your broker; Real-time data flux is essential. The subscription to the Eurex data flux (DAX and mini DAX) will cost you about 20 euros per month and another 25 euros for a subscription to CME CBOT (e-mini Dow) data. Your broker collects the fees for the data supplier; you don't need to pay the supplier directly. If you just want to trade CFDs, you won't have to pay these fees, but you will have only access to the data provided by your broker.

Most of the platforms will let you place simple orders such as buy limit or sell limit orders, with the option to set up an automated take profit and stop-loss orders. But some go even further by letting you set up an automated order for part of the position and another one for the second part of the position and so on if you want to set up 3 different targets.

Be aware that some brokers operate with a first-in-first-out rule, which means that they won't let you have opposite positions on the same product run separately, a.k.a. hedging. A new executed sell order may not open a position but offset or close an already opened buy position. On the other hand, CFD brokers may let you trade, hedge, and operate your positions separately from one another. While short and long positions of equivalent quantities and on the same product offset each other in theory, your broker may still calculate a margin cover for each position separately. So, keep an eye on your margin usage.

If you are starting with a small account, i.e., with less than € 5,000, look for brokers that will let you trade on small quantities, as small as 1/100th of one lot. That way, you can start trading taking minimum risk until you build confidence in your trading.

Being able to trade from a smartphone, an iPad, or similar. I certainly cannot recommend that you use these devices for your scalping, but they shall be used as part of plan B if a problem comes up with your computer while you are trading or if your internet broadband suddenly shuts down or resets itself. Your smartphone connected to a mobile phone network will be your back up device to modify or close some orders if necessary, until your computer and the internet are back up and running. Most brokers offer mobile technology in today's world.

This was plan B. The plan C is that you should be able to call your broker's trading desk as a last resort in case of emergency if your computer and your mobile application don't let you perform an action that needs to be done.

Lastly, you absolutely need to work with a minimum of two brokers because if for any reason, there is a technical problem on one of your brokers' platforms, you need to able to act swiftly on your second broker's platform. Let's say you need to close a position, but broker A's platform, for some reason, is not working. Then you can always open an opposite order on the broker's B platform. For instance, you need to close a long position with broker A, but a technical problem doesn't let you do so. Then you should open a short position with broker B until everything is back up and running. Then you can work on closing these positions simultaneously afterward.

Once you are ready to trade with the mini futures, I recommend that you have at least 12,000 euros to be able to scalp with 2 lots when the occasion occurs. For the most accurate information, choose the tick by tick data flux if you can choose a data provider. Some data providers offer market data sent to your computer on a second by second basis while others have their data refreshed on a tick by tick basis, which is every time a transaction occurs on the market, showing you the latest price exchanged.

The choice of broker that you go for is crucial to your trading success. Conduct proper research on the best broker to work with. Some qualities of a good broker include:

- They are regulated by a relevant monetary body.

- They offer all the instruments that you need to trade.

- They are cheap in terms of commissions and other charges.

- They are reputable in all aspects.

- They are accessible any time you need them.

- What are your strengths and weaknesses?

Finally, you must evaluate yourself and see which of your traits make you a better trader and which ones limit your potential. Identifying your strengths will keep you motivated, and you will pay more attention to your stronger side. On the other hand, identifying your weaknesses will allow you to know what needs some improvement. You will become a better trader as you work on more of your limitations.

These are just some of the elements that you can include in your trading plan. You can add more as you please, as long as they add value to your trading career. The most important thing, however, is that you follow the rules in your constitution to the end. If you only compose it and stop at that, it will be as good as seeing a good trade setup and letting it go.

Chapter 3:
Futures Spread Trading

Many day traders find futures preferable to options because they are sure to always move along with the asset that they are related to. What's more, the futures market can be analyzed directly, which means that you can profit from anticipation on the market without having to take any derivative pricing into account. Even better, unlike some other markets, there are no artificial restrictions limiting your ability to short trade, making your job as a day trader much easier in the process. Finally, this makes it so that the FINRA's definition of a pattern day trader does not apply. A pattern day trader is required to keep $25,000 on hand at all times, among other things, and being labeled as one will make it more difficult for you to trade as effectively as possible.

- **Always follow the trends:** Odds are, if you are attracted to futures trading, then you are less naturally inclined to follow trends in the market, preferring instead to jump in on opportunities when they are still forming. This is a habit that you are going to need to break if you plan on trading in futures; however, typically, you will find that the practice is much more profitable if you stick with the trends of the major players and deviate from them as little as possible.

- **Don't prioritize trade frequency:** While it is natural for day traders to make more trades than other types of traders, that is no reason to assume that there are always future trades that can be made at the moment. It is important to always keep in mind that it is possible to be a successful day trader while making three trades a day, just as it is to be successful while making 30 trades per day. It is all about choosing your futures targets carefully and with a clear understanding of where all the trades are likely headed. Don't forget, before you finalize any trade, you should always run a full risk/reward analysis to ensure that it is going to be worth your time in the long run.

- **Know what a good futures contract looks like:** Prior to starting any trade, it is important that you take the time to gather as much information as possible in order to ensure you prevent any further surprises from sneaking up unannounced. It is important to keep in mind that futures contracts may have a number of key differences that will need to be considered before moving forward. First, it is important that you know the contract unit in question as each potential futures contract will show the size as well as the units it is trading in. Forex futures will always be specified with a given currency, while those based on stock indices generally include a reference point on the index multiplied by a specific price per share. The specifics of this measurement aren't as important in most instances as they are generally only crucial in the moment to help you understand exactly what you are getting yourself into. Outside of these types of specifics, you will need to keep in mind the quoted price as well as how this quote is likely to change between markets as sometimes, they will be written with dollars and cents while other times they will be written with mathematical equations, possibility points or percentages. The end result will always work out to be the same, but it is important to know exactly what you are working with prior to moving forward.

- **Choosing the right contract:** Prior to choosing the right contracts to follow, it is important to understand the various levels of insecurity that are taking place in the market in question compared to the potential for a serious payout should things go just right. This is vital as there is a great deal more variance in the futures market than in the others as they encompass a far greater variety overall. When it comes to making these types of decisions, it is also important to remember that past performance is not going to be an accurate predictor of future results in this instance. This means that just because a price has remained stable for several days is no indication that it will continue to do so.

- **Look for the right signals:** When day trading futures, it is important to keep in mind that the best results will typically materialize if you use a trio of indicators that aren't specifically corollary to one another. You will need to keep an eye on the sine wave as a means of determining the price when it comes to support and resistance, the momentum to determine the volume in comparison to the supply, and the pro-am as a means of determining the specific trade size to help determine how much interest the market has in the trade at the moment. Generally speaking, you can expect to have the ability to plot the sine wave through the lowest chart pane, which will give you a measure of the current cycle. When levels of support and resistance are both confirmed, you will see the results mapped via dotted lines on the price bars in question. You will also find the momentum plotted underneath the bars indicating price, and it will then be represented by waves to show the volume when it comes to buying and selling. You will also find various divergence patterns that can then be directly plotted onto various additional price bars as well. When it comes to tracking the pro-am, you will be able to easily consider what types of active traders are sitting on various price points. If you find a lot of highs, then you can be confident that it means there is lots of position switching taking place at the top of the spectrum. Meanwhile, lots of lows should tell you that the breakout is on its last legs, which means it could likely reverse at any time.

- **Consider the direction the trend is forming:** More so than in more traditional forms of trading, if you manage to find a trend while day trading, then there is a high chance that you will be able to successfully make a profit off of it, assuming it sticks around long enough to let you. When it comes to confirming the direction of a potential trend, you will want to take note of professionals who are trading in the space before confirming that the trend is set to continue on moving forward as well. You will want to keep an eye out for indicators that it has reached a point where its volume is exhausted, as this means it is likely on its last legs.

- **Stick with a single market:** While the futures market tends to have various subsections devoted to various different markets, this doesn't mean that you should bounce between them all as you will have far more success if you stick to those which you see some early success. Once you have mastered a specific subsection of the market, you can then move on to the next, but until that point, you will want to focus on the way you can increase success in the long-term.

Futures Spreads Trading Pricing and Margins

Spreads

It is vital that you keep in mind that if they are part of a spread, then the individual margins on a given contract will be reduced. For example, if the margin on a given wheat contract alone is $2,000, but if you make the decision to go short as well as long on wheat in the same year, then the margin between them could potentially be as little as $200. If you go short and long on one commodity split over different years, then the margin will double to $400. The price differential occurs as the volatility of the spread is less than that of the contract in question.

Generally speaking, the futures spread gives you the ability to look at the given market movement in slow motion. Thus, if something major happened in the wheat market, then it would affect both contracts, which would provide enough protection against the increased risk that the singular contract doesn't have.

Price Concerns

The price of a specific futures spread can be easily determined via the perceived difference in two contracts. To properly determine what the spread's pricing is going to be, the easiest way to go about doing so is to simply find the pricing of the spread by just subtracting the month that is being deferred from the price of the front month. If the price of the front-month is the lower of the two, the spread will end up being negative, and if it is higher than the spread, it will end up being positive. The values for the contracts, as well as the spreads, will remain the same. For example, if the price of wheat is $500 in the front month and $510 the next, then the spread can be said to be -$10, and if it instead dropped to $490, then it would be $10.

Market Types

Contango Markets

A market is thought to be contango if the front month is going to clearly have a lower cost than the deferred month. Generally speaking, this means the deferred month is going to cost slightly more than the front month will, thanks to the cost to carry. The cost to carry will take into account the interest rate on the capital that comes along with the operating costs of the location that actually sells the commodity in question, as well as any related storage or insurance costs. This is considered the default state of the market.

Backwardation Markets

A market is said to be in the midst of backwardation if the near months are valued more highly when compared to the months that are the deferred month. Sometimes known as an inverted market, it is the opposite of the standard market condition. This most commonly occurs if the market is in the midst of a bull phase, which tends to be caused by a supply chain issue, often in relation to a substantial increase in demand along with an overall limited supply. This type of price differential typically occurs when the front months feel the full brunt of the change, which is then mitigated as the deferred months start arriving. This is frequently the case if the deferred month ends up in the next crop year after the front month.

Regardless of the state of the market at the moment, it is important that you always factor seasonal concerns into all of your choices as well. Generally speaking, you can count on gasoline prices being higher in the summer while prices of coffee, natural gas, and heating oil will be higher in the winter. Furthermore, it is important that you remember all markets will inevitably experience bearish and bullish periods, but those experienced by commodities tend to be far less consistent overall.

Common Spread Types: Commodity Futures

Inter-commodity Futures

These futures involve contracts that are spread across various markets. As an example, if you believe that the wheat market is going to experience a high demand when compared to the corn market, then you would buy wheat and sell corn. The specific prices for each don't matter as long as wheat prices beat corn prices.

Calendar Intra-commodity

This spread looks at a single commodity between differing months of the year. As an example, if you believe that the wheat market is going to be stronger in November as opposed to June, then you would go long in November and short in June. The specifics of the price don't matter as long as prices are higher in November than they are in June.

Bull Futures

This spread looks at a single commodity under the assumption that the sooner month will boast a higher price than the later month. As an example, if you buy a bullish wheat future in May, then you will want the price to be higher than when you sell it in June. For this type of future, it is important to keep in mind that near future contracts tend to move faster the further you get from the front month, which gives this future its name. A bullish trader would then be one who buys in the front month in hope that it ends up moving at a greater rate than the deferred month.

Bear Futures

This spread occurs if you purchase the same commodity in such a way that you are short in the front month and long on the deferred month. As an example, if you purchase wheat in May and sell it in June, then you are hoping the prices are lower in May than they will be in June. For this type of future, it is important to keep in mind that near future contracts tend to move faster the further you get from the front month, which gives this future its name. If you are confident that prices are at a low point, then this is the type of spread you should consider buying into.

A pattern day trader is required to keep $25,000 on hand at all times, among other things, and being labeled as one will make it more difficult for you to trade as effectively as possible.

Chapter 4:
How to Make a Profit on the Futures Market

When to Trade and When Not to Trade

The markets go through different phases, and there are times when you will feel like it is difficult to read the market or other times when there are low volumes and high hesitation from market participants making the market evolve in a flat and boring momentum.

DAX future, 5 minutes

For this example, I have used 5-minute candles in order to fit the whole day on one chart. As you can see, the market makes roughly 60 points between its lowest of the day and its highest of the day, which is not too bad. But how did that happen? A rapid 30 points drop in the morning, followed by a return to opening prices by the end of the morning, and then, 6 hours of long awaiting until a little awakening again at 5 pm. Apart from doing mini range trading during these 6 hours, there is not much you can do.

It is difficult to predict how a day is going to be. I am not talking about trends here, but just about price volatility. Is it going to be an active day or a very quiet day? You can't really know in advance. However, there are some hints that you can look for, such as previous day's behaviors and chart patterns.

DAX Future, One Hour

When the market is testing significant levels such as supports and resistances, you can expect some hesitation as no one is willing to buy at the highest and push the market further until an event or something triggers the market to make a breakthrough or consolidate sharply. When reaching significant levels and testing them, expect the market to test that level before breaking it or reversing it.

Another hint to look for market activity can be found in the economic calendars and how the market is reacting to the coming events or news to be announced. The market may enter into a quiet phase, with fewer participants willing to trade, waiting for the news to be released. Some participants will indeed decide to stay on the side, as I will advise you to do next. During this quiet phase, the volumes exchanged could be low, again due to the fact that many day traders don't want to have too many positions opened while facing the risk of high price volatility at the time of the news being released. You should get familiar with the average volume exchanged throughout the day for the product you are trading so that you can assess if the market is being pushed around in low volumes by fewer participants or if indeed there is increased interest.

When scalping, you may want to close all your positions before the news is released because the market might get very volatile on and after the news is being released. While volatility normally serves us, at the time of a news release, the market can move erratically in any direction, come back to where it was before the news went out, or set up in a specific direction. What will happen is that you may have traded in the right direction, but the market went to hit your stop-loss first due to price volatility. Now, you may say, let's not put a stop-loss in this instance or place it further away, but what happens if the market goes against you and then doesn't reverse in your chosen direction? Placing orders just before the news is released, from my point of view, is just gambling. Don't try to apply logic to the market's reactions to the news either, thinking that if the news is positive, the market will certainly go up or the opposite because it may not happen. The market may already have priced the news with some market participants starting to cash in their profits making the prices go in the opposite direction of where they should logically have gone. When news or a figure is released, you don't have all the information around it. For instance, if crude oil inventories are lower than forecast, is it due to higher oil consumption or lower oil production? What strategies do the market participants have in place? Many factors and many questions for which we don't have all the answers to be able to analyze the news and predict how the market is going to digest the news. Sometimes, following a news publication, the market reacts strongly by going one way but recovers in the next two hours and resumes its current activity. So, don't try to gamble on the news. With experience, however, you will get to know when important news are likely to have no impact on the market at particular times while they may be strongly scrutinized at other times.

The main macro-economic news that often impacts the markets are interest rates decisions from central banks and their press conferences, crude oil inventories, American employment, inflation figures, GDPs, and home sales. Depending on the context, they may trigger volatility when released.

You can find calendars with news release dates and times on many websites. I like to use the economic calendar published on investing.com and apply a filter to show the major news.

Economic Calendar

As the week is finishing, I look at the following week's events and report them to my computer calendar and save reminders and alarms that go off one hour to 30 minutes before the news release. That way, it reminds me not to open any more positions just before a news release and close existing positions while in positive territory.

Below is a list of additional times when I recommend not trading:

The first ten minutes after the stock market opening: I am talking about stock market opening and not futures market. During the first ten minutes, the market can move in different ways, not giving us useful readings. Indeed, some participants may be closing positions they didn't manage to close the previous day or for which they had sufficient margin at that time but no longer. Other participants may open or close positions due to their option hedging work, and so on. Different traders with different agendas. The first ten minutes may create volatility that again may trigger scalpers' stop-losses without giving any opportunity to the scalper.

The triple witching day: this is the name given to the day when, on a monthly basis, index futures contracts, stock index options contracts, and single stock options contracts expire; even quadruple witching day when single stock futures contracts add to this list on a quarterly basis. Triple witching day takes place on the third Friday of the month and quadruple witching day on the third Friday of the month every quarter-end. Volumes become artificially higher due to positions being rolled over to the next contract term. Volatility may also increase as market participants have different agendas, but it may not help the scalper, so I choose to take it easy these days.

The last day of the quarter: Some market participants may be at work to improve their balance sheet and quarterly reporting. However, don't start thinking that it will trigger an uptrend because if rising prices may improve the balance sheet of institutional investors, it may have an adverse impact on those with short positions in their books.

Holidays and festive seasons: during those times, volumes are lower. The market may be in a free-spinning mode or move rapidly in low volumes. If you absolutely want to trade, do it on lower volumes because when institutional investors and big market movers are on holiday, the market may not give you the right opportunities to realize good trades.

Trading after 10 pm: Mini DAX and DAX futures are not tradable after 10 pm, but for the e-mini Dow, CME lets the trader carry on their trading on an OTC system via its GLOBEX platform. So, if you really want to trade e-mini Dow non-stop, you can start at midnight on Monday until 11 pm on Friday (these hours can change slightly during the winter and summertime changes). However, trading after 10 pm is not recommended because the volumes are likely to be very low. Focus your energy instead on the US pre-market opening, which is at 14:30 CET.

Trading the Mini-DAX and DAX Pre-market Opening

Mini DAX and DAX futures markets open at 7:50 am one hour and 10 minutes before the stock market opening.

Most of the time, pre-market opening is very quiet with low volume transactions. No need to rush to your screen and start trading at 8 am. However, when the market made a strong move the day before, there may be opportunities arising in the pre-market opening. We know that market participants have different agendas, but when the market reacts strongly in one direction, it can put speculators in difficult positions. For instance, if the market went down by 300 points in one day, some long traders may face margin calls meaning they will have to either put more cash in their account or close some of their positions. This will lead to more sell orders being put on the market. At the same time, some sellers may want to cash in and close winning trades. In the first minutes of pre-market opening, you won't know how the market will evolve, but you can certainly use the Heikin Ashi candles to perform some trades because after a strong move the day before, there is likely to be volatility in the pre-market opening.

DAX, One Minute: 300 points is a strong intraday move for the DAX.

Quiet pre-market opening has prices that move within a ten to twenty-point range. But here, after a strong move on the previous day, we can expect some volatility.

The Most Effective Method to Make Money Trading Futures

Exchanging fates is a type of contributing that can give broadening to a portfolio and assist you with overseeing hazard. Fates contracts apply to agrarian wares, rising and falling as the market interest of things, for example, corn, steel, cotton, and oil change. You can make cash exchanging fates on the off chance that you pursue patterns, cut your misfortunes, and watch your costs.

Follow Trends

Fates markets have patterns, much the same as different protections markets do. Items tend not to have a similar unpredictability as stocks; however, it can likewise be less unsurprising. At the point when you distinguish a pattern through thorough research and testing, it speaks to your most obvious opportunity to benefit. Research includes investigating which components sway the organic market of the item that you're keen on. Testing includes making mimicked interests in prospects that you think you see slants in to see whether a genuine venture would have worked out.

Cut Losses Short

Any individual who puts resources into fates long enough is going to buy gets that lose esteem. On the off chance that a specific agreement begins to move in opposition to your desires, firmly consider undercutting and assuming a little misfortune. The option might be trusting that the agreement will ascend in esteem, just to see it fall further. Since each agreement you purchase is with the desire that it will see gains inside your time skyline, stopping misfortunes by selling will expand the arrival that you return to contribute somewhere else and counterbalance different additions when you ascertain salary venture for your charges.

Margins and Expiration Dates

Financial specialists exchange fates on edge, paying as meager as 10% of the estimation of an agreement to possess it and control the privilege to sell it until it lapses. Edges consider duplicated benefits, yet additionally profit you can't stand to lose. Keep in mind that exchanging on an edge conveys this unique hazard. Select gets that terminate after when you anticipate that costs should arrive at their pinnacle. A March prospects contract is pointless on the off chance that you get it in January yet don't anticipate that the product should arrive at its pinnacle an incentive until April. Regardless of whether April contracts aren't accessible, a May contract is increasingly proper since you can sell it before it lapses yet hold up until after the ware's cost gets an opportunity to rise.

Brokers and Expenses

Financial specialists exchange prospects contracts through conventional representatives just as online agent administrations. Online administrations offer less customized exhortation but, at the same time, are more affordable, offering exchanges for under $1 now and again. Utilize an online specialist and play out your own market investigation to minimize expenses and increment your net addition from exchanging fates. Track all costs, including intermediary charges and memberships to on the web or print productions that help you contribute, to deduct them as speculation costs on your annual expenses.

Most Significant Hints on the Best Way to Profit in the Fates Advertise

Try Not to Attempt the Fates Advertise on the Off Chance That You Have No Cash

Many individuals get the possibility that creation cash on the prospects trade is simple, and they feel free to put enormous sums on that they can't stand to lose. That is a major NO.

Try Not to Attempt Some Trick or Mystery You Read in a Book

The fastest method to lose cash on the fates showcase is to go out and attempt one of the mysteries you got notification from a companion or read in a book. These are simply gossipy tidbits and, for the most part, don't work. In the event that you are going to test a specific methodology, guarantee you do it relaxed and with modest quantities of cash before going hard and fast. Little tests will assist you in seeing reliable results. You won't profit, yet the dangers are little, and you won't lose your whole record on the off chance that things conflict with you.

Think Present Moment and Long Haul

Try not to attempt to make sense of what will occur in the fates showcase in the following 2 hours. Indeed, this can profit; however, there are a ton of effective merchants that are making cash long haul in fates moreover. They couldn't care less about the every day variances or what happens each moment consistently.

Don't Over Investigation

There is such an incredible concept as making a decent attempt on the fates trade. Regularly the great merchants will discover something that works and, afterward, continue attempting to make the framework and procedure work better. Simply acknowledge, there is no sacred goal to exchanging. There is no framework that is going to profit 100% of the time. Acknowledge you will take little misfortunes, and discover a framework that works reliably and stick to it. Keep it near you and use it as your weapon against the market.

Utilize an Expert Exchanging Stage

There are numerous great stages you can use to exchange prospects. In any case, there is a darker side to exchanging prospects, where numerous broking houses offer carriage stages that are more regrettable than inferior. Simply do your schoolwork first and discover what the top dealers are suggesting. These stages ordinarily play out the best and keep customers cheerful. At the point when it is your cash in danger, you need to guarantee you have well-being and dependability on your side. Generally, there can be radical outcomes.

Know What's Going on Out There in the Economy

After the worldwide money related emergency, a few nations are doing ineffectively, and there is, at present, a few monetary standards issues. It may merit your opportunity to discover how the economy is getting along in your general vicinity of the world. In the event that things are not looking great, it is smarter to set aside cash to purchase day by day things before you go gambling everything on the fates advertise.

Utilize a Demonstrated Stop Misfortune the Board Framework

This is the main motivation behind why numerous merchants out there come up short. They toss cash into the fates advertise without pondering what their arrangement is if things conflict with them. Things won't work out as expected 100% of the time. Taking misfortunes are a part of the game and increasingly like a cost of doing business for proficient brokers. Simply acknowledge it and consistently leave a position on the off chance that it conflicts with you. It is difficult to concede you aren't right, yet simply acknowledge it and get out of the exchange. That will guarantee you have cash for the following exchange that presents itself.

Exchanging Knowledge for Success in the Futures Market

Greatness Is a Result of Difficult Work

Appropriate exchanging information is the way to accomplishment in the prospects advertise. You can go right back to the Bible, and it will advise you about the significance regarding shrewdness. Adages reveal to us that shrewdness is the rule thing, and to go get insight and comprehension. The entirety of the incredible brokers and financial specialists from the beginning of time took a stab at securing the information important to get world-class. This is the manner by which they made fortunes exchanging the different markets. There is no easy route to turning into a world-class broker.

Study and Learn as Much as You Can

In the event that you need to make progress in the prospects showcase, you essentially should place in the time and exertion important to secure the best possible exchanging information. Achievement originates from knowing and following demonstrated fixed guidelines. The individuals who need information normally surmise or pursue the counsel of TV characters. This is a sure catastrophe waiting to happen.

Do Not Put Together Your Exchanging Choices with Respect to Feelings

Probably the greatest misstep new brokers, and even experienced ones make, is to be affected by feelings, for example, dread, insatiability, and expectation. One approach to cure this is to execute an effective exchanging plan that accommodates your character. On the off chance that you just pursue flag legitimately from your arrangement, it will assist you with trading just on certainties and not feelings. Try not to belittle the significance of appropriate exchanging brain science. It is a significant piece of your general exchanging information that will prompt achievement in the prospects advertise.

Charts Will Give You Extraordinary Data

On the off chance that you appropriately study the value developments and volume on a diagram, they will reveal to you more about what is happening than any investigator, TV character, or merchant. Diagrams are an incredible wellspring of previous history, with pieces of information to future value developments.

Following an unmistakable pattern is one of the significant keys to making a great deal of cash exchanging the different markets. On the off chance that a market is in an exchanging range, have the tolerance to hold up until it unmistakably breaks obstruction or backing. At that point, float along with the market. Try not to avoid the pattern. Make sure to consistently rehearse sound cash the executives. This can be accomplished by deliberately putting stops following you take a position. When the market goes your direction, actualize trailing stops to ensure benefits. You should rehearse sound judgment through the whole procedure. This originates from appropriate exchanging information and experience. You can turn into a reliable victor in the fates showcase or the financial exchange.

Tips for Intermediate Futures Options Traders

As a futures trader, you should make sure that you understand very clearly what a short position is and a long position is. There are plenty of novice traders who believe that you only make money or are profitable when markets are on an upward trend. However, you need to understand that futures trading constitutes a lot more than just following the upward market trend. You also should know by now that as a futures trader, you can benefit greatly when you focus on asset types that have attained a climax and are close to failure.

As a trader, anytime that you wage your money against an asset, then you will be said to be selling it short. Selling an asset short simply means that you will engage your broker and purchase the rights to access the asset with the hopes of selling it back later once it becomes profitable. Using this analogy, we can purchase apples at the market for $1 each and then selling them back at $2 each, making a profit of $1.

In real life, this $1 can be exponentially multiplied to earn you large sums of money. This is the way futures markets work. You stand to make large sums of money from simple trades.

Long Positions

As a futures trader, you are ready to invest your funds in a particular asset when you take a long position in it. In this situation, you will only benefit from this position when the price of the asset rises. As a futures trader, you need to be able to determine whether and when an asset is likely to rise in price. This determination requires you to learn about the fundamentals of the asset. For instance, how is the supply and demand in the market? Being able to answer such questions with a high level of accuracy will enable you to decide whether to invest in it or not.

Basically, each asset market has its own rules that help interested parties, including traders, to provide intrinsic value as well as the determination of momentum, both negative and positive. The Central Bank is the premier institution when it comes to currency, so currency traders need to take note of the policies and statements released by this institution.

In this instance, currency fluctuations sometimes depend on interest rates. If you anticipate a rate hike, then it is advisable to go long on the specific currency. Higher interest rates should provide a suitable incentive to hold long an asset. This way, there will be increasing demand for the currency, and you will be able to eventually sell at a great price and make lots of profits.

When it comes to stocks and other instruments, it is corporations that drive their value. For instance, the earnings report will determine the value of a company's stock in the short and long terms. Earnings reports are often released quarterly. During these events, company executives reveal their earnings for the past three months as well as their forecasts for the future. Therefore, if a company announces a reduction in production, closure of a store or plant, and so on, then you should assume a long position. The reason is that reduced production will very likely result in higher prices within a couple of months.

Short Position

When it comes to short positions, there are plenty of similar factors compared to long positions at play but in reverse. Therefore, factors or elements that cause you to choose a long position will, in reverse, determine a short position. For instance, if you are interested in currency and there are signs of reduced inflation, then you may want to take a short position on the currency.

Basically, when there are signs of declining inflation, central banks may decide to lower interest rates in order to provide a stable financial position in the markets. On the other hand, when interest rates are high, then as a futures trader, you will want to take the path that all other futures traders do. When interest rates are high, products and services are generally expensive for the consumer.

Costly products mean lower sales figures, and this will mean reduced incomes for corporations and so on. As such, it will be appropriate for futures traders to sell short because of the high-interest rates. Some of the instruments that can be sold include shares and stock indices. Commodities markets and their instruments also operate in the same manner. When there are high-interest rates at play, the markets tend to experience low demand. Commodities such as gold and oil will then most likely begin selling short at the markets.

Basically, it is advisable to have a good idea regarding factors that are actually negative and which ones are considered positive, especially with regards to your preferred asset. This way, you can do your research and analysis to determine if you are to sell an asset or buy.

Intermediate Futures Trading

It is often difficult for traders with small accounts to make any significant gains in the futures market. As an intermediate trader, you do not need to be too concerned about this. This is because you can use leverage to overcome your small account size challenges.

Leverage provides an effective pathway that enables you to capitalize effectively on your positions. Leverage also provides a reliable pathway that will enable you to increase your profit potential as you maximize your positions in the trade. This means that you will be able to leverage in a manner that allows you to profit in numerous ways not otherwise possible.

Leverage can help you maximize your gains. However, be extremely cautious because leverage can also compound your losses should you incur any. It is possible that your analysis could travel in the wrong direction. When this happens, you could incur some losses, and these could have an impact on your account. You could, for instance, receive what is known as a margin call. When this happens, you will be required to fund your trading account. Should you not be able to fund your account due to losses, then it will be shut down.

Things That Distinguish Winning and Losing Traders in Options Trading

As an options trader, you need to know how to calculate and find the break-even point. In options trading, there are basically 2 break-even points. With short term options, you need to make use of the commission rates and bid spread to work out the break-even point. This is if you intend to hold on to the options until their expiration date.

Now, if you are seeking short term trade without holding on to the options, then find out the difference between the asking price and the bid price. This difference is also known as the spread.

Embrace the Underlying Stock's Trend

As a trader, you should learn to jump successfully on a trend and follow the crowds rather than go to extremes and oppose it. Most amateurs who see an upward trend often think the stock is about to level out. However, the reality is that the momentum is often considered a great thing by seasoned traders. Therefore, do not try and oppose the trend because you will surely lose.

Instead, try and design a strategy that will accommodate the trend. In short, the trend is always your friend, do not resist as momentum is great.

Watch Out for Earnings Release Dates

Call and put options are generally expensive, with the price increases significantly if there is an earnings release announcement looming. The reason is that the anticipation of very good or very bad earnings report will likely affect the stock price. When this is an underlying stock in an options trade, then you should adjust your trades appropriately.

Once an earnings release has been made, then options prices will fall significantly. You need to also watch out very carefully about this. The prices will first go up just before the earnings are released and then fall shortly thereafter. It is also possible for call options prices to dip despite earnings announcements. This may happen if the earnings announced are not as impressive as expected.

As an example, stocks such as Google may rise insanely during the earnings announcement week only to dip significantly shortly thereafter. Consider Apple shares that were trading at $450 at the markets. Call options with Apple as the underlying stock were trading at $460. However, the market had targeted a price of $480 within 3 days, which did not happen. This costs investors' money. Such underlying assets are considered volatile due to the high increase in price, rapid drop shortly thereafter, and a related risk of losing money.

Traps to Avoid on Expiration Day

The ease of the guidelines for participation and the aggressive marketing brings a lively interest of people for the binary options trade. Some greedy brokers take advantage of this desire that touches an audience of new private investors, mostly beginners. The most frequent abuses or frauds found are:

- **The impossibility of withdrawing your money:** Here, the fraudulent binary options broker prevents any withdrawal or does not accept withdrawals until a minimum level is reached in the account.

- **Fraud in the bank card:** Once the bank details are sent (by phone or after a first deposit), withdrawals are made from the client's account without their authorization.

- **An offer of "bonus" is offered to the clients:** The company commits to credit in the customer's account the same amount as this deposit. The client then learns that the bonus is not granted until "bet" at least x times its amount (20 to 30 times in the cases cited).

- **Fraud in managed accounts:** Training offers are proposed, and a "coach" is assigned to the client. Very often, the coach proposes to the debutants to be advised by telephone in their bets. When the first losses occur, the coaches advise the client to place supplementary funds to "redo." When losses accumulate, "the coach becomes unplayable or gives the only explanation that a bad operation is the source of the losses."

- **Conditions of trade impossible to achieve:** The broker demands the investor to make positions more than x days in the month. Maybe even more than the number of days worked in the month.

- **Withdrawal penalty:** The broker applies significant "charges" from 10 to 50% to dissuade the investor from recovering their money. Generally, the merchant has no knowledge of this information until the day he tries to withdraw his funds and has a hard time finding this information before.

On the other hand, if the most serious companies propose access to a market resulting from supply and demand, the majority is happy proposing over the counter products (without going through a stock market). The prices are then decided either by the company itself, which acts as a counterpart for its own account and has an interest in the client losing, 5 either by an affiliated company or friend.

Chapter 5:
Golden Trading Rules and Mistakes to Avoid

Stock trading is becoming more popular each day. This is basically the most preferred monetary resource by individuals to generate money. Just about every other person or family discusses it.

There are a few fundamental principles for successful stock trading that are implemented persistently by successful traders.

Of course, if you follow these rules as well, you will probably become successful and make money with stock trading.

It is crucial to read through these effective stock trading rules before you decide to get into the stock market, regardless of whether you're a beginner or even an expert.

Trend Is Your Friend

Go long if the stock is bullish and go short if the market is bearish. Never go against the trend. Stick to this vital rule for successful stock trading.

Always Plan Your Trade

Use a proper trading plan to ensure success; that should include a position, the reasons you enter, stop-loss level, profit taking level, along with a sensible money management approach.

Protect Your Capital

Establish a limit for your trading and protect your money. Do not place beyond 10% of your portfolio in one trade. If you do not abide by this stock trading rule, you will likely be out of the market soon.

Don't Extend Losses

In case the trade goes against you, get out of that position and do not hesitate over it. If you hang on for too long, assuming that the price will increase, you will simply end up losing more money. Settle on your stop-loss price level before you actually enter a trade.

Don't Be Greedy; Take a Timely Profit

Once the trade seems to be in profit, book some of that profit. Select how much profit you are prepared to take. Sit back and watch the profit run by adhering to this rule for successful trading. Buy climbing stocks and sell dropping stocks.

Leave Emotions Out of the Trading Ring

Greed and fear are often the two most significant emotions in trading. Do not allow these to have an effect on your trading. Any successful trader is usually emotionally consistent.

Keep Your Trading Record

Whenever you trade a stock, it will help to write down the main reasons why you bought or sold, as well as your emotions during that time.

Evaluate afterward and write down the errors you made, along with the right choices you made. One more successful stock trading rule would be to keep studying and improving.

Don't Listen to Others

Trade only depending on your personal study and analysis. Steer clear of trading based on what your friend or other people are saying. A properly informed trader constantly marches forward.

If in Doubt, Then Do Not Trade

If you are unclear about the trend in the market, keep away. You should not disregard this particular rule for successful stock trading. It can help you achieve a lot by not doing anything.

Overtrading Is the Real Enemy

You must not have more than 3–5 positions at any given time. Several positions could make you lose control and make incorrect sentimental choices. Therefore, never trade just for the enjoyment of trading.It requires plenty of discipline to harvest large profits and guide your journey to the stock trading achievements. So look at the previously mentioned rules for successful trading before you actually get into the stock market, even if you are a profitable stock trader.

Holding Positions Until the Subsequent Day Is Risk

Going long on futures, holding positions long can presumably cause you to lose money. The futures may shut at the tip of the day at one value and open the resulting day at a fully completely different value.

Traders who exclude their positions daily do not have to be compelled to worry about losing money once the market opens in the morning. This method could also be an important transaction strategy.

Choose a Liquid Market to Trade

Before you start to trade futures, study the little print of each market. With this, you may build the foremost effective selection. You need to be trained and be careful to attain success in commerce futures. Once new traders begin to be told plenty of and gain some experience, it's simple to form mistakes that can cause problems associated value an excessive quantity of money. A number of those mistakes embody making risky trades and commerce you may afford. You need to be cautious and organized to succeed in the trade.

Settling of Contract

Trading futures contracts do not involve the immediate delivery of assets. Subsiding of contract happens solely on the date that it expires. Traders can even settle before the contract's expiration if they like better to do, therefore.

Don't Stay on the Trend, Follow It

The hardest suggestion for a trader is to follow trends. Traders are independent individuals who do not appear to belong to the group or part of the herd.

Follow a System, Don't Get Into Chaos

Be very clear about the reasons why you need to introduce futures trading techniques if you want to reach the milestones you need to achieve.

Possible futures trading techniques have to do with making clear possible market fluctuations in the coming year. If you're not clear, don't expect to go too far shopping.

Accept Losses, Adjust Gains

Another key is simply to adjust your losses and gains. Learn how to trade from the small side and watch out for divergences in online shopping. Staying out is as important as entering the markets. Patience could be a virtue.

Have a Healthy Business Plan

This includes a clear understanding of entry and exit points, value targets, risk-reward relationships, attitudes, knowledge of historical value levels, seasonal influences, graphical analysis, cost-related markets, and government reporting. Don't expect to make a profit.

The impetus for mercantilism is out

A disciplined system of business selection is important. Being impulsive instead of objective will cost you more than one operation. Swap with inspiration instead of relying on emotions. Find out how to deduct profits, decide the risk of trading on margin, and anywhere to boost market circulation.

Discipline Is Essential

You have a tight schedule for each operation that can change unless thorough knowledge supports it. Disciplined cash management involves smart transaction allocation as well as risk management, and once you create a thriving transaction, don't worry about the success of the successful transaction.

Keep in mind that the future career of commercialism is a kind of chess game. You can only survive if your next move is sweet enough.

Volatility Is Often Explosive

The airline business is a double-edged sword. You cannot simplify it if you decide on difficult decisions an unstable financial process that will form. Keep in mind when calculating the odds/reward ratio before choosing a trade and beware of the risk of keeping it for a long time.

Follow an Idea, Think About the Future

Once a controller is established, and stops are selected, don't choose until the stop or the main reason for changing the controller is reached. Use technical analysis to maintain discipline and not compromise emotional objectivity.

Not Timing the Market Correctly

While everyone is familiar with the old adage buy low and sell high, it doesn't translate particularly well into practical advice. Many investors who attempt to buy low when they think the market has bottomed out or try and sell when the market is at an apparent peak often lose out those to those investors who simply purchase reliable pairs and hang onto them for the long term. What's worse, many of those who attempt to time the market end up losing lots of money, which can be devastating, depending on how heavily they were invested in the scenario.

Making Investments That Are Too Risky

It is important to keep in mind that the further you are from retirement, the riskier of investments you can make as you will have more time to recover if you choose poorly.

However, once you are within 5 years of retirement, it is always going to be better to take the safer investment with the lower estimated return than it is to invest in anything even remotely risky. A good rule of thumb when it comes to determining how much of your overall portfolio could be in forex is to take your age and subtract that number from 110. The result is the percentage of your portfolio that should be based around stocks.

Making Investments That Aren't Risky Enough

If you are closer to retirement, then the greater mistake is making investments that are too risky; if you are further away from retirement, then the greater mistake is not taking enough chances. When you have plenty of breathing room between now and your retirement, it is important to take advantage of this fact to the fullest and take greater risks to help maximize your earning potential while you have enough time to mitigate the additional risk. If you are currently in your thirties, then a full 80% of your portfolio could be in the forex market without issue.

Not Knowing Your Limits

It is certainly possible to enter into retirement without having to micromanage your finances. But in order to do so, you are going to need to plan for a less complicated retirement strategy prior to retirement, something that few people take the time to do. This will require meeting with a financial advisor and taking their advice to heart, again, something that not nearly enough people do. You should meet with a financial advisor and then again about five years before you retire, just to ensure you are on the right track. Be sure you have the basics of your retirement investment plan outlined before you go and listen to any of the suggestions they make. After all, you only get to retire once; it is best to make it count.

Being Overconfident

Many people believe that they are smarter than the market as a whole, which means they can be the odds, even if the odds are very, very low. If you don't think this is the case, then consider how many people play the lottery on a regular basis. If you are someone who plays the lottery on a regular basis, it is important to be aware of this propensity and avoid betting more than is rational when it comes to individual trades.

The fact of the matter is that most people are going to be average, at best, when it comes to trading in the forex market. What this means is that you are going to want to do everything in your power in order to mitigate this average performance when it comes to trading.

Never Only Look for Information That Confirms What You Already Believe

If you are dead set on trading in forex pairs that you choose yourself, it is important to do as much research as humanly possible before committing to anything. After all, even if you still have plenty of time before you need to start changing a majority of your holdings away from forex, you never want to throw your money away. As such, when you are doing your research, it is important to look at all of the available data, not just that which conforms to the ideas you have about an existing stock.

Don't Resort to Anchoring

Anchoring is the term given to irrationally being stuck on a specific number for a specific trade without having any real reason for doing so. The same thing can happen to those who hold onto a specific pair for too long and miss a profitable sale point in the process. Or worse, if you are holding onto a currency that you bought at $5, which then drops to $3, an anchoring mindset will cause you to hold onto it despite conventional wisdom saying it is better to cut your losses before it drops even further.

The most efficient way to avoid an anchoring bias is to ensure that you have a firm trading plan in place with buy and sell points determined before you make a commitment. Knowing what you are going to do before you do it is a great way to ensure that your emotions don't get in the way and to prevent you from anchoring without even realizing it.

Accept That Loss Is a Part of the Process

The forex market runs on risk. This is a fact and cannot be changed, no matter how much you wish; this might be the case. Risk drives price and is ultimately responsible for any profits that you make in both the short and the long term. With this fact in mind, it then becomes much easier to deal with loss and respond to it accordingly. While this doesn't mean that you should take unnecessary risks, it also doesn't mean that you should hold onto losing propositions simply because you don't want to accept the loss.

Putting All Your Eggs in One Basket

While there is a difference between investing and trading, traders can learn a few things from our investor brothers (and most people are a little of both anyway). Don't let everything ride on one trade.

If you take all the money you have and invest it in buying options for one stock, you're making a big mistake. Doing that is very risky, and as a beginning trader, you're going to want to mitigate your risk as much as possible. Betting on one stock may pay off sometimes, but more times than not, it's going to lead you into bankruptcy territory.

Investing More Than You Can

It's easy to get excited about options trading. The chances to make fast money and the requirements that you analyze the markets can be very enticing. Oftentimes that leads people into getting more excited than they should. A good rule to follow with investing is to make sure that you're setting aside enough money to cover living expenses every month, with a security fund for emergencies. Don't bet the farm on some sure thing by convincing yourself that you'll be able to make back twice as much money and so cover your expenses. Things don't always work out.

Going All in Before You're Ready

Another mistake is failing to take the time to learn options trading in real-time. Just like getting overly excited can cause people to bet too much money or put all their money on one stock, some people are impatient and don't want to take the time to learn the options markets by selling covered calls. It's best to start with covered calls and then move slowly to small deals buying call options. Leave put options until you've gained some experience.

Failure to Study the Markets

Remember, you need to be truly educated to make good options trades. That means you'll need to know a lot about the companies that you're either trying to profit from or that you're shorting. Options trading isn't possible without some level of guesswork, but make your guesses educated guesses, and don't rely too much on hunches.

Not Getting Enough Time Value

Oftentimes, whether you're trading puts or calls, the time value is important. A stock may need an adequate window of time to beat the stock price, whether it's going above it or plunging below it. When you're starting and don't know the markets as well as a seasoned trader, you should stick to options you can buy that have a longer period before expiring.

Not Having Adequate Liquidity

Sometimes beginning investors overestimate their ability to play the options markets. Remember that if you buy an option, to make it work for you, you're going to need money on hand to buy stocks when the iron is hot. And you're going to need to buy 100 shares for every option contract. Before entering into the contract, make sure that you're going to be able to exercise your option.

Not Having a Grip on Volatility

If you don't understand volatility and its relation to premium pricing, you may end up making bad trades.

Failing to Have a Plan

Trading seems exciting, and when you're trading, you may lose the investor's mentality. However, traders need to have a strategic plan as much as investors do. Before trading, make sure that you have everything in place, including knowing what your goals are for the trades, having pre-planned exit strategies, developing criteria for getting into a trade so that you're not doing it on a whim or based on emotion.

Ignoring Expiration Dates

It sounds crazy, but many beginners don't keep track of the expiration date. Would you hate to see a stock go up in price and then hope it keeps going up, and it does, only to find out that your expiration date passed before you exercised your option?

Over-leveraging

It's easy to spend huge amounts of money in small increments. This is true when it comes to trading options. Since stocks are more expensive, it's possible to get seduced by purchasing low priced options.

Giving in to Panic

Remember that you have the right to buy or sell a stock if you've purchased an option. Some beginners panic and exercise their right far too early. This can happen because of fears that they'll be missing out on an opportunity with a call option or because of fears that a stock won't keep going down on a put.

Chapter 6:
Proven and
Time-Tested Futures Trading Strategies

Fundamental Trading

This is where you have to do research into the markets in which you want to trade, read the daily press reports on weather conditions, study information like supply and demand figures, agricultural reports and economic news, etc. This takes up an excessive amount of time and money and is mainly used by large institutional investors with the necessary resources to do all the research.

Technical Trading

With this method, you make use of charts to analyze the movement of the markets, also known as Technical Analysis.

It is much more suited for the small trader. It does not require having to make decisions based on a lot of subjective information.

Comparing and Combining Models

The data you are looking for is in Table 19.1, where the strategies that we looked at earlier are listed, as well as the same statistics for the S&P 500 Total Return Index, all covering the backtesting period from the start of 2001 to the end of 2018.

Table 19.1 Futures Strategies Statistics

	Annualized Return	Max Drawdown	Annualized Volatility	Sharpe Ratio	Calmar Ratio	Sortino Ratio
trend_model	12.12%	-25.48%	19.35%	0.69	0.48	0.98
counter_trend	11.00%	-30.09%	18.55%	0.66	0.37	0.92
curve_trading	14.89%	-23.89%	18.62%	0.84	0.62	1.22
time_return	11.78%	-40.31%	21.09%	0.63	0.29	0.9
systematic_momentum	7.84%	-39.83%	16.48%	0.54	0.2	0.76
SPXTR	5.60%	-55.25%	18.92%	0.38	0.1	0.5

Clearly, the curve trading model is the best one, right? And the momentum isn't worth bothering with? Well, conclusions like that are the reason why I did not show these simple statistics earlier. Evaluating trading models is a more complex undertaking than simply looking at a table like this. You need to study the details and study the long-term return profile. And, of course, scalability. At the sharp end of the business, you often look for a specific behavior in the return profile, often relative to other factors. The answer to which model is more promising depends on what you happen to be looking for at the moment and what would fit or complement your current portfolio of models.

All of these models are simple demo models. They are teaching tools, not production-grade models. But they all show potential, and they can be polished up to become production grade models.

You can also see that all of them are orders of magnitudes more attractive than a buy and hold stock market approach. Some readers may be surprised to see just how meager the return of the stock markets is over time. In this period, from 2001 to 2018, the S&P 500 returned less than 6% per year, even with dividends included and even with the last ten years of bull market included. And that was at a peak drawdown of over half.

Another point that may surprise some is the level of the Sharpe ratios. None are over 1. There is an unfortunate misconception that a Sharpe of less than one is poor. That's not necessarily so. In fact, for systematic strategies, it's unusual to see realized Sharpe ratios of over one.

Comparing Futures Models

Shows the long-term development of these five strategies, compared to that of the stock market. On such a long-time scale, the index comparison hardly seems fair. But the fact is that in the shorter run, you will always be compared to it. This is the curse of the business.

Remember that the reason that these backtests start in 2001 is that a current, and hopefully soon addressed the issue in Zipline makes it tricky to use pre-2000 data. The fact that the equity index starts off with a nosedive might make this comparison a little unfair, and for that reason, I will also show you the same graph starting in 2003, the bottom of the bear market. I won't do one from the bottom of the 2008–2009 bear market. That would just be plain silly. Comparing perfect market timing into the longest-lasting bull market of a generation with alternative strategies does not make any sense. Comparison, starting from 2003.

Even if we would have had the foresight of buying the index with impeccable timing at the bottom of the tech crash, the index would still have shown lower return and deeper drawdowns.

Combining the Models

Everyone knows that diversification is beneficial. At least everyone should know that. But most people think of diversification only in terms of holding multiple positions. That's all fine and well, but you can also find added value in diversifying trading styles. Think of a single trading model as a portfolio component.

What you may find is that an overall portfolio of models can perform significantly better than any of the individual strategies that go into it. I will demonstrate this with a simple portfolio consisting of the five trading models we have seen so far.

As we have five models, we will allocate an equal weight of 20% of our capital to each. The rebalance period is monthly, meaning that we would need to adjust all positions accordingly each month, resetting the weight to the target 20%. Such a rebalance frequency on a model level can be both difficult and time consuming for smaller accounts but is perfectly reasonable on a larger scale. Feel free to repeat this experiment with yearly data if you like. Making portfolio calculations like this is an area where Python shines compared to other languages.

Table 19.2 Portfolio of Futures Models

	Annualized Return	Max Drawdown	Annualized Volatility	Sharpe Ratio	Calmar Ratio	Sortino Ratio
trend_model	12.12%	-25.48%	19.35%	0.69	0.48	0.98
counter_trend	11.00%	-30.09%	18.55%	0.66	0.37	0.92
curve_trading	14.89%	-23.89%	18.62%	0.84	0.62	1.22
time_return	11.78%	-40.31%	21.09%	0.63	0.29	0.9
systematic_momentum	7.84%	-39.83%	16.48%	0.54	0.2	0.76
Combined	14.92%	-17.55%	11.81%	1.24	0.85	1.79

Table 19.2 shows a comparison of the performance of each individual model, as well as the overall stock market, to that of the combined portfolio. These numbers should be abundantly clear. The combined portfolio far outperformed each individual strategy,

at lower volatility. We got a higher annualized return, a lower maximum drawdown, lower volatility, higher Sharpe, etc.

You may find a model with a low expected return over time, but which also has a low or negative correlation to other models, and thereby can greatly help your overall combined portfolio of trading models.

Portfolio of Trading Models

As the individual models often have their gains and losses at different times from each other, they complement each other well and help smooth out long term volatility. The drawdowns become subdued, resulting in a higher long-term return.

While it was a close call some years, in the end, not a single year of this combined portfolio ended up losing money.

Table 19.3 Holding Period Analysis for Combined Model

Years	1	2	3	4	5	6	7	8	9	10	11	12	13	14	15	16	17	18
2001	8	13	17	18	17	16	18	19	19	20	18	17	17	17	17	16	16	15
2002	18	22	22	20	17	19	21	20	21	20	18	18	18	17	16	16	15	
2003	27	24	21	17	20	21	21	21	20	18	18	18	17	16	16	15		
2004	21	18	14	18	20	20	21	19	17	17	17	17	16	15	14			
2005	15	11	17	20	20	21	19	16	16	17	16	15	15	14				

Year												
2006	7	18	21	21	22	19	17	16	17	16	15	15	14
2007	29	29	26	26	22	18	18	19	17	16	16	14	
2008	29	24	24	20	16	16	17	16	15	14	13		
2009	20	22	17	13	14	15	14	13	13	12			
2010	25	16	11	12	14	13	12	12	11				
2011	8	5	8	12	11	10	10	9					
2012	1	8	13	12	10	11	9						
2013	16	20	16	13	13	11							
2014	24	16	12	12	10								
2015	9	6	8	7									
2016	4	8	6										
2017	13	7											
2018	2												

Implementing a Portfolio of Models

While a demonstration like this may seem to show a simple solution to all your investment vows, an implementation may not be as easy. Each of these models requires millions to trade. Clearly, trading them all requires even more millions. I recognize that not every reader of this book has a spare hundred million laying around to be traded. But even if you are one of those unfortunate few non-billionaires out there, understanding the power of combining different approaches can be greatly helpful.

As the complexity rises, you lack the simple overview, which is possible with a single model, and you may need more sophisticated software to keep track of positions, signals, risk allocation, etc.

A professional trading organization can build the capability of trading such complex combinations, to monitor the risk and build proper reporting and analysis. For individual traders, this may not be a possibility.

Of course, there is another way to look at it. An understanding of how complex portfolios of models can be constructed and implemented can help you acquire the skillset needed to land a good job in the industry. Working at the sharp end of the industry has the potential to earn you far more money than you could possibly make trading your own portfolio.

Never forget that the interesting money in this business is made from trading another people's money. Whether or not you personally have the money to trade such models is not the important part. Well, it would be nice to have that, of course. But you can still make use of this kind of knowledge, and you can still profit from it. If you land a good job with a hedge fund or similar, you will probably get paid far more by working for them than you could by trading your own money anyhow.

Support and resistance

Understanding support and resistance is crucial to achieving the success you are looking for when it comes to technical analysis. While they may seem complex at first, they will become clearer every time you put the theory around them into practice. At their most basic, resistance can be thought of as the ceiling on the price of a particular currency or currency pair, which means the price is unlikely to move past this point. In contrast, support can be thought of as the price floor, which is unlikely to decrease further.

Understanding the concept of support and resistance is key to the success of your trading. Just about all timing approaches are based on buying near support levels and selling near resistance levels. Support is a certain price level where buying pressure is greater than selling pressure, and resistance is a price level where selling pressure is greater than buying pressure. The 18 and 40-day moving average is a great tool to use to indicate support level on a correction during an uptrend. Prices often find their support level at the 18 and the 40 days moving averages, which means that buying pressure will outweigh selling pressure at such levels and that the prevailing trends are likely to resume again from these levels. The same holds true when the market is in a downtrend when we also will find the resistance at the 18 and 40 days MA levels.

Previous highs and lows can also act as support and resistance levels. Earlier lows tend to slow the declining of the price down because many traders believe that the price previously rallied from these levels and can do so again. Such traders are likely to go long or cover their shorts at these levels. If the price slips below the old low, then the role of this price level is reversed and becomes the new resistance level. The reverse happens when the price reaches old highs.

Moving Averages

Of all the indicators Moving Averages (MA) are probably the most basic and well-known indicators. Moving averages are a way to define a trend mathematically.

A moving average can be constructed by adding up the closing price of a certain number of days and then dividing the total by that number of days. Then each day, the oldest price in the series is dropped, and the most recent close is added. But you don't have to worry about calculating moving averages because they are available on most charts anyway. What is important is to know how to use them.

The most commonly used is the 4, 9, 18, and 40-day moving averages. The 40-day moving average is a great tool to use to determine the direction of the medium-term trend. A flat or horizontal 40-day moving average line reflects a sideways market or a phase between trend reversals. When the 40MA is sloping upwards, it means the intermediate trend is up, and the reverse is true when the 40MA is sloping downwards. To confirm an uptrend, make sure that the 9-day MA is greater than the 18-day MA and the 18-day MA greater than the 40-day MA. Confirmation of a downtrend means that the 9-day MA is smaller than the 18-day MA and the 18-day MA smaller than the 40-day MA.

Trend Lines

While it is not uncommon for these ceilings and floors to change regularly, being prepared for these changes is what separates the novice traders from the experts. Understanding these movements is done through the use of trend lines. When the market is trending upward, new resistance levels will be formed as that upward price movement begins to slow before starting its trek back down the trendline. This is likely to happen when uncertainty rises with a given stock. This will, in turn, create what is known as a short-term top, which is essentially a temporary price plateau in the overall movement pattern.

Shorter trends can be part of trends that are much longer overall, which is why it is important always to double-check and ensure you aren't making a move on something that is only an offshoot of a much larger and much different trend. To decide what's even easier, it is important to always keep an eye on the weekly, daily, and yearly charts if you want to locate any truly long-term trends. If you are looking to get rich quick, you will want to stick to the daily charts instead.

After you have found an especially interesting trend, draw a straight line that correctly illustrates the direction the trend is currently moving in. When it comes to an uptrend, you will want to draw your line in such a way that it connects the dots of all of the lows in such a way that the line is below the relevant data. If you are looking at a reversal trend, you will want to draw the line so that it connects the highs, leaving the data below the trendline.

It is important to start paying extremely close attention to the price of the stock that you are watching when it begins to reach again the point where the trendline begins to broaden as this is likely to be the point where the price is going to cease its downward fall. It is important to note in instances such as this that a trendline can lend support to a given stock for a significant period while changing very little in the interim. Likewise, if the market is in a downward trend overall, then you will want to be on the lookout for a set of peaks at a declining angle and a trendline that connects the point of each peak. As the price gets closer to the trendline, you will want to be on the lookout for indicators that point towards selling, as this is how the price was likely pushed lower previously.

You will also want to keep an eye out for channel lines, a pair of lines to the side of the data you are watching that indicate the levels of resistance and support in play. One trendline connects the highs while the other connects the lows. At the same time, the resulting channel can either go up or down, or even sideways, but the interpretation will always remain constant. The goal should be to establish a long enough channel to show a break from the data that it has been following. This breakout point will mark the best time to get in on the trend you are following to ensure that you have the maximum amount of time to profit from the trend you have discovered.

Chapter 7:
Technical and Fundamental Analysis

Technical Analysis

Technical analysis is ideal for determining future performance by looking at previous prices without having to dig through mountains of paperwork to find the details you are looking for. While the past will never be able to predict the future 100% of the time truly, technical analysis is useful when combined with a basic understanding of market mentality for generating predictions that are accurate within reason.

You have embarked on a very exciting journey into the profitable world of technical analysis. I will walk you through the core concepts of charting and show you how to time your trades with precision.

When it comes to understanding technical analysis, the most important thing to always keep in mind is that the action that a certain price has taken in the past is likely going to be a reliable way to predict its action in the future. This fact then makes it easy to use what are known as technical tools, things like indicators, charts, and trends to achieve a reliable rate of success that successful traders require. While the ways it can do so can be quite complicated at times, at its heart, technical analysis studies supply and demand in an effort to decide what trend, if any, is likely going to continue moving forward. This is crucial for long term success as the tools that technical analysis provides will increase the reliably of each of your trades nearly every single time.

The goal of technical analysis is not to simply measure the given intrinsic value of a particular asset but rather to use the tools at your disposal to pick out beneficial patterns related to a future activity that others may not yet have noticed.

Who Uses Technical Analysis?

Speculators like us who are looking towards making big profits, Professional fund managers' very livelihood depends upon making other people rich, Hedgers or commercials are the people who actually own the physical commodities. In short, all market participants who demand a professional edge. This tells us only one thing—if the professionals use technical analysis, it must be very important; before we get to really good stuff, it's important to understand why technical analysis works.

Core Assumptions

The goal of technical analysis is not to measure the given intrinsic value of a particular currency but rather to use the tools at your disposal to pick out beneficial patterns related to a future activity that others may not yet have noticed. At its core, technical analysis functions by assuming three things to be true. First, the market will always discount anything; second, prices will always move according to trends; and finally, history will always repeat itself eventually.

The Market Will Always Discount Everything

Detractors say that technical analysis is only concerned with the movement of currency price and little else in reality. Technical analysis assumes that the current price of a currency reflects everything that is going on that could affect that currency, which then makes it an accurate way to assess overall value. This is taken into account along with the broader economic climate as well as the current phase to determine when a valuable opportunity comes along.

The Price Will Always Move According to Trends

If the current value or price of a given currency is said to move according to an established trend, you can determine a trend in past currency performance. You have a much greater chance of seeing that same trend repeat itself when compared to the chances of an entirely new trend or the opposite trend occurring instead. Technical trading strategies tend to assume that this is always the case if they are going to work effectively.

History Will Repeat Itself Eventually

If prices move in trends, then it naturally stands to reason that technical analysis believes that as far as currency prices go, history will always repeat itself. This can be chalked up to the fact that those who participate in the market are likely always to respond the same way to similar market movement. This is often plotted using chart patterns to determine these trends at their start when they can be capitalized on to the fullest. While some of these charts have been in use for over a century, they are still relevant when it comes to how the public reacts to price changes.

Price Charts

A price chart is a core part of technical analysis; essentially, it is a chart with both an x and a y-axis where the price can be seen along the vertical axis. The time can be seen along the horizontal axis.

While there are plenty of different charts to choose from, each with their unique strengths and weaknesses, you will want to keep in mind early on, including the line chart, the candlestick chart, the bar chart, and the point and click the chart.

Line Chart

The line chart is the simplest of all the charts because all it does is showing the closing price of a given stock over a set period. In this case, the lines are formed once the grouping of closing prices has been determined and then connected with the end goal of showing a trend. You won't be able to find details such as what the opening price for the same period was or what the overall results for the day were. However, you will be able to determine if the day over day is positive, which is still quite important, which is why this is one of the first charts that day traders of all skill levels consult when they are looking into the details of new stock.

Candlestick Chart

Another worthwhile technical analysis tool that you want to be familiar with is the candlestick. They provide important data for traders across multiple time frames by creating what is known as price bars. Each day will provide you with details regarding the high, open, close, and low stock points each day. These details can be used to build patterns that make it easier to predict how the price is likely going to move in the future.

The candlesticks that are going to be the most accurate when it comes to plotting the price of stocks are going to fall into two types, continuations, and reversals. Reversal candlestick patterns tend to predict a coming change in the current pricing trends. Meanwhile, continuation patterns predict that the current price action is simply going to continue as is.

A candlestick chart is similar to a bar chart, though the information it provides is much more detailed overall. Like a bar chart, it includes a line to indicate the range for the day. However, when you are looking at a candlestick chart, you will notice a wide bar near the vertical line, which indicates the degree of the difference the price saw throughout the day. If the price that the stock is trading at increases overall for the day, then the candlestick will often be clear, while if the price has decreased, then the candlestick is going to be red.

Point and Figure Chart

While the point and figure chart aren't used as much as it once was, it has been in use for more than 100 years, which means there is still plenty of use left in it. The point and figure chart are useful when you want to know the movement of prices, without worrying about volume or time spent. This makes it a pure pricing indicator without much of the noise that many other charts need to deal with. It is also useful if the other types of charts contain information that skews them in one way or another.

When you first see a point and figure chart, you will always be able to tell because it comprises lines of Xs and Os instead of points and lines. In this instance, the Xs will indicate periods of positive trends, while Os will represent downward trends. The numbers and letters along the bottom of the chart indicate months and date estimates. Point and click charts also include a set of reversal criteria set by the trader looking at the chart; these criteria consider the amount the price is going to move for an X to become an O or vice a versa. As the trend changes, it shifts right to indicate this fact.

Bar Chart

A bar chart expounds upon the details provided by a line chart by providing a greater degree of detail regarding the specifics of the day. The top and bottom of the bar represent the high and the low for the day, respectively, while the price at closing is indicated on the ride side of the bar with the help of a handy dash. The dash on the left side of the bar shows the starting price, while the color of the bar indicates if it experienced an overall increase or decrease by the end of the day.

How to Read the Main Tools and Charts

Each futures contract has a unique one-or two-letter code assigned to it that identifies the contract type. Futures codes or ticker symbols are used by the exchanges to process all trading transactions. For example, the symbol for corn is C, while the mini-sized corn future is YC. It is imperative to use the correct code when you trade; otherwise, you can end up trading the wrong contract.

In addition to the contract code, you must also know the month and year code. The month code J represents April and K represents May etc. So, if you want to trade the May corn futures in 2011, the code would be CK5. See Month Codes Chart below:

It is imperative to understand a contract's value. This is how you will determine the profit and loss as well as the entry and exit price when you trade. Futures contracts have a minimum price increment called a tick. Traders use the word tick to express the contract movement or amount that a market has moved up or down.

Another term you will have to understand is the term "multiplier," which determines the value of a tick. For example, the multiplier for the Canadian dollar is $10. The market moved up by 20 ticks in one day. This means your long contract has gained $200 (20 ticks X $10.00 multiplier = $200).

Contract Codes and Specifications Chart

Full Contracts			
Contract	Delivery	Contract	Minimum

Corn	C	H,K,N,U,Z	5,000 bu.	¼¢/bu = $12.50
Oats	O	H,K,N,U,Z	5,000 bu.	¼¢/bu = $12.50
Soybeans	S	F,H,K,N,Q,U,X	5,000 bu.	¼¢/bu = $12.50
Soybeans Meal	SM	F,H,K,N,Q,U,V,Z	100 tons	10¢/ton = $10.00
Soybeans Oil	SO	F,H,K,N,Q,U,V,Z	60 000 lbs	.01¢/lb = $6.00
US T-Bonds	US	H,M,U,Z	$100,000	1/32 = $31.25
US T-Notes 10yr	TY	H,M,U,Z	$100,000	1/32 = $31.25
US T-Bonds 5yr	FV	H,M,U,Z	$100,000	1/64 = $15.625
Wheat	W	H,K,N,U,Z	5,000 bu.	¼¢/bu = $12.50
Australian Dollar	AD	H,M,U,Z	AD100,000	.01¢/AD = $10.00
Canadian Dollar		H,M,U,Z	CD100,000	.01¢/CD = $10.00

British Pound	BP	H,M,U,Z	BP62,500	.02¢/BP=$12.50
Eurodollar	ED	H,M,U,Z	$1000,000	1pt. = $25.00
Euro	EC	H,M,U,Z	€ 125,000	.01¢/€ = $12.50
Feeder Cattle	FC	F,H,J,K,Q,U,V,X	50,000lbs.	2.5¢/cw=$12.50
Japanese Yen	JY	H,M,U,Z	JY12,500,000	.0001¢/JY=$12.50
Lean Hogs	LH	G,J,M,N,Q,V,Z	40,000 lbs.	2.5¢/cwt = $10.00
Live Cattle	LC	G,J,M,Q,V,Z	40,000 lbs.	2.5¢/cwt = $10.00
Live Hogs	LH	G,J,M,N,Q,V,Z	40,000 lbs.	2.5¢/cwt = $10.00
Mexican Peso	ME	H,M,U,Z	MP500,000	.0025¢/MP=$10.00
S&P 500	SP	H,M,U,Z	$250 x Index	0.05 = $12.50
S&P Mini	ES	H,M,U,Z	$50 x S&P index	0.25= $12.50

Swiss Franc	SF	H,M,U,Z	SF125,000	.01¢/SF=$12.50
US T-Bills	TB	H,M,U,Z	$,1000,000	.01 = $25.00
Cocoa	CC	H,K,N,U,Z	10 metric tons	$1/ton = $10.00
Coffee	KC	H,K,N,U,Z	37,500 lbs.	.05¢/lb =$18.75
Sugar #11	SB	H,K,N,V	112,000 lbs.	.01¢/lb = $12.00
Cotton	CT	H,K,N,U,Z	50,000 lbs.	.01¢/lb =$5.00
Orange Juice	JO	F,H,K,N,U,X	15,000 lbs	.05¢/lb =$7.50
Copper	HG	All Months	25,000 lbs.	.05¢/lb = $12.50
Gold	GC	G,J,M,Q,V,Z	100 troy oz.	10¢/troy oz = $10.00
Silver	SI	H,K,N,U,Z	5,000 troy oz.	.005¢/troy oz = $25.00
Mini Contracts				
Corn	XC	H,K,N,U,Z	1,000 bu.	¼¢/bu = $2.50
Soybeans	XS	F,H,K,N,Q,U,X	1,000 bu.	¼¢/bu = $2.50

US T-Bonds	YH	H,M,U,Z	$50,000	1/32 = $15.625
US T-Notes 10yr	XN	H,M,U,Z	$50,000	1/32 = $7.8125
Wheat	XW	H,K,N,U,Z	1,000 bu.	¼¢/bu = $2.50
Eurodollar	UD	H,M,U,Z	$500,000	.005 = $6.25
Feeder Cattle	FM	F,H,J,K,Q,U,V,X	10,000 lbs	.001 = $10.00
Lean Hogs	HM	G,J,M,N,Q,V,Z	10,000 lbs	.001 = $10.00

Fundamental Analysis

In order to successfully trade in the futures market, one of the most important things you are going to need to learn is how to determine a reliable way to tell a potentially profitable trade from one that is likely to fizzle out or, even worse, cost you money.

Fundamental analysis is used more frequently by new traders, while technical analysis has experienced something of a renaissance in popularity over the past decade or so. While both are useful when it comes to finding the information you are looking for, they go about determining just what that information is in different ways. Fundamental analysis is primarily concerned with looking at the big picture, which often means that it will take longer to perform than its counterpart.

Also, its information comes from external sources, which means you may need to wait for additional information to become available through it will typically end up being easier to digest than the information required to utilize technical analysis effectively.

Broadly, the fundamental analysis makes it easier for you to glimpse the likely future of the futures market based on a wide variety of different variables, including publicized changes to the monetary policy of the countries you are interested in. The end goal is to track down enough information to allow you to find an undervalued currency pair that the market has not adjusted to.

Determine the Baseline

When it comes to considering the fundamental features of a currency pair, you will first want to consider the baseline that these currencies typically return to time after time when compared to the other currency pairs that are commonly traded. This will make it easier to determine when the right time to make a move is likely to be, as you will then be more easily able to pinpoint changes that occur to the pair that make them warrant additional consideration.

In order to determine this baseline, the first thing you will need to consider is any changes to the related macroeconomic policy that affects each based on historical data. In these instances, past behavior is one of the most reliable indicators when it comes to determining likely future events. Once you are aware of the relevant historical context, you will then need to consider the current phase the currency is in and how likely it is to remain in the phase-in question as opposed to moving on to the next.

Each currency regularly goes through 6 distinct phases, the first of which is the boom phase, which can be identified via low volatility and large amounts of liquidity. At the opposite end of the spectrum is the bust phase, which can be identified by the opposite, mainly low amounts of liquidity and high amounts of volatility.

The other phases are post-bust and pre-bust and post-boom and pre-boom, which means that one of the major phases is either on its way in or on its way out. Determining the proper phase is crucial when it comes to ensuring that you are on the right track when it comes to finding a trading pair that is likely to be profitable in the long-term.

In order to determine the current phase, the easiest way to go about doing so is by looking at the current number of defaults along with bank loans as well as the accumulated reserve levels of the related currencies. If the numbers are low, then a boom phase is likely on its way or possibly in full swing already.

If the current numbers have already overstayed their welcome, then you can be confident that a post-boom phase is likely to start at any time. Alternatively, if the numbers in question are higher than the baseline you have already established, then you know that the currency is likely either due for a bust phase or is already underway.

Money can be made regardless of the current phase as long as you can capitalize on it before the market catches up, as it is typically fairly slow-moving. The earlier you can pinpoint the coming phase, the greater the dividends you can expect to see are going to be.

Worldwide Considerations

After you have an understanding of the baseline, the currency pairs you are working with tend to remain at; the next thing you will want to do is to determine is what the related global economic conditions are likely to be and how they are going to affect your trading pair.

In order for this to be effective, you are going to want to look beyond the obvious signals and dig deep to find the indicators that are surely going to make waves after they become public knowledge. One of the best ways to go about doing so is to looking into emerging technologies in the related countries as they can easily turn entire economies on their heads in a relatively short period of time.

Technological indicators are a great way to use a boom phase to its full advantage as by getting in on the ground floor, you can ride the wave for as long as it takes for that technology to become a full-fledged part of the mainstream. After it reaches the saturation point, you are going to want to be on the lookout for the bust phase, as it will likely be right around the corner.

If you feel as though the countries related to the currencies in question will soon be in a post-bust or post-boom phase, then you will want to think twice about moving into speculative markets as the drop off is sure to be coming, and it can be difficult to determine exactly when it will rear its ugly head.

If you feel confident that a phase shift is on the horizon, but you don't know when it will be exactly, then you are going to want to stick with smaller leverage points than you would during the other phases to ensure that they will pay out before the change occurs.

On the other hand, if a phase is just starting, then you will want to go ahead and make riskier trades as the time concerns aren't going to come into play, which means extra caution is less warranted.

Global Implications

While regional concerns are a good place to start, it is also important to take a macro view of the market as a whole, as global currency policies are almost always likely to play a part in the proceedings.

While it might be difficult to determine where you should start, at first, all you really need to do is to apply the same level of analysis that you have performed on the micro-level, just on a larger scale. The best place to start is generally going to be with the interest rates of the major players on the world stage include the Federal Reserve, the European Central Bank, the Bank of England, and the Bank of Japan.

You will also need to be aware of any policy biases of legal mandates that are currently making the rounds in order to ensure that you don't end up getting blindsided from these sources when it comes time for you to make your move.

While this will certainly be time-consuming work, understanding the market from all sides will make it easier to determine new emerging markets when specific areas are fat with supply growth and what the expectations regarding interest rate changes or market volatility are soon going to be.

Understand the past: After you have a clear idea of what the current state of the worldwide economy is looking like, along with the specifics regarding the currency pairs you are interested in trading, then the next thing you will need to do is look to the past so that you can be prepared for history to repeat itself.

This level of understanding will make it easier for you to understand the current strength of your respective currencies while also allowing you to more accurately determine the length of time you can expect the current phase to continue.

In order to capitalize on this knowledge in the most effective way possible, you are going to want to attempt to jump onto trades when one of the currencies is entering a post-bust phase while the other is in the midst of a post-boom phase.

When this occurs, credit channels will not yet be exhausted, and you will be able to take advantage of the greatest amount of risk possible when compared to any other market state.

Be Aware of Volatility

Being aware of the current level of volatility is crucial when it comes to ensuring that the investments you are making are likely to actually payout in your favor. This is relatively easy to do; all you need to do is to pay attention to the stock markets most closely related to the currencies you favor.

This is because the futures market tends to be more stable. The more stable the stock market is, the lower the perceived overall risk is, the lower the amount of perceived risk that can make its way to the futures market.

Remember, the closer to the peak of the boom phase you currently find yourself, the lower interest rates, default rates, and volatility will be, which means it is the best time to increase your level of risk. Alternately, the closer you find yourself to the bust phase, the higher the overall level of volatility, default, and interest rates are going to be.

Decide on the Best Currency Pairs

With a good idea of where the market currently is and how long it is likely to stay there, all that you have left to do is determine the most effective currency pairs to actually sell. To do this, you must first consider any gap between the 2 currencies when it comes to interest rates. You need to have a clear understanding of where each of the pairs is currently and how likely they are going to remain close together and with a proper distribution between them.

To find this information, you are going to want to start by looking at the difference in the output gap as well as related unemployment statistics. When capacity constraints increase, while at the same time, unemployment decreases, this shortage will lead to an inflated economy, which in turn, will cause interest rates will rise until the economy begins to cool. Charting this information will allow you to accurately determine the likely interest rate movement from the pair in question.

Also, you will want to consider the payment balance of the nations related to the currencies in question. The healthier the debt to capital ratio, the stronger the related currency is likely to remain in times of crisis. To determine this amount, you are going to want to consider the capital as well as the current account and the general situation of each.

This will help you to determine if the position the nation in question is holding is due to asset sales or bank deposits or other, long-term potential developments, including things like an accumulation of reserves or foreign investment.

Economic Indicators to Watch

When it comes to major economic indicators, the list is a fairly short one. Unfortunately, if you hope to stay competitive in the futures market, then you are going to need to keep up with far more than just the basics.

This is easier said than done; however, as there are a huge variety of economic surveys and other relevant indicators that can be used to predict numerous types of trends before they happen. While the entire list is too massive to include in its entirety, the options listed below will get you started on the right track.

Beige Book

More formally known as the Summary of Commentary on Current Economic Conditions by Federal Reserve District. This is because, rather than simply present the reader with raw data, it instead uses a tone that is much more conversational as it describes the various regional goings-on of the various members of the United States Federal banking districts.

This allows traders to determine how the Fed comes to various conclusions in various circumstances, which, in turn, can be useful later on when it comes to making bets on how the currency will move in the future. This economic indicator is published prior to each Federal Open Market Committee Meeting, which works out to be 8 times per year.

While the beige book does not typically create that much of a commotion as it doesn't present anything strictly new. Instead, it helps to point knowledgeable traders in the likely direction that things are going to be moving in the future. For example, if the overall tone of a beige book indicates a growing worry about inflation, then you might be able to start making preliminary plans related to a decrease in the current USD interest rate.

Consumer Price Index

A consumer price index is a sort of benchmark for a specific country's economy and its current level of inflation. It utilizes a basket approach as it attempts to compare a steady base of products that don't change much from year to year. These products include many common items, including toiletries and other common groceries, in addition to everyday services like the price of a haircut or an oil change.

These numbers tend to be broken down into a handful of figures, the first of which is broken down into two categories known as the Urban Wage Earners and the Clerical Workers. The second category is known as Urban Consumers. The consumer price index for a given set of urban consumers is often tracked quite closely as it varies dramatically throughout the year.

In the US, the current percentage is shown in comparison to the year 1982, so changes can only be determined based on previous index levels. Numbers are then shown via a run rate of growth to show traders what they can expect from inflation as well.

Meanwhile, the chain-weighted consumer price index often sees a major push when it comes to relevancy. This index provides a numerical visualization of customer purchasing patterns when compared to other indexes. As an example, only the chain-weighted index notes, things like when the public shifts from one brand to another based on things like price increases.

In addition to major economic indicators like these, the consumer price index is often viewed by many trades as the final say when it comes to the up to date financial situation of a given country. It is released once per month, and when it is, you can count on serious movement for any related currency pairs.

Durable Goods Report

This report is released monthly and provides valuable updates when it comes to the amount of manufacturing that is being done in a given country when it comes to durable goods. A durable good is any type of capital goods that has an average lifespan of more than three years. Nearly 100 different industries fall under this report's purview, including things like cars, semiconductors, and even wind turbines.

The figures for a given country will be provided in the currency of that company along with a percentage of change for the month over month numbers. Three months of revisions are also included in every report. Data from this report is one of the 10 core components of the US Conference Board Leading Index, which is used to divine futures movement in the global market.

When it comes to reading these reports, it is vital that you always remember that the numbers that are publicly reported often do not include transportation goods or items created by the defense sector as they tend to be volatile enough to skew things dramatically one way or the other. Thus, if you want the full story in a given country, you will need to do your due diligence and sniff these numbers out for yourself.

Generally speaking, the durable goods report is an excellent way for savvy traders to get a viable overview of business demand in specific countries. This is the case because these types of capital goods tend to require a larger overall investment, which, in turn, shows that business owners and consumers are both acting with greater confidence than they would be if the economy was not moving in a positive direction.

Based on the results you find, you may also find it especially useful to consider topics like the variation that occurs when it comes to inventory and shipment ratios over a prolonged period of time, in addition to the growth rate of shipments and related inventories.

Taken together, these should provide a much clearer picture of whether or not supply is exceeding demand or vice versa. As these types of goods often take far longer to be created than more transient goods, the durable goods report can also be an excellent way to get an early read on the expected earnings increases for the future month as an influx of orders in one month is a good sign that additional growth will be forthcoming.

Employment Cost Index

The employment cost index is a useful economic indicator that is released four times per year. It focuses on the amount that businesses in a given country pay for each employee, on average, as well as how much that has changed over the preceding quarter.

This report looks at things like employee benefits, hourly wages, bonuses, and any relevant employee premiums for every industry besides government and farm labor, as these would skew the numbers at either end of the spectrum.

This data is then broken down on an industry by industry basis before being split even further based on whether or not the industry is unionized. This information tends to also be broken down industry by industry, which makes it especially useful to traders who are looking for early indicators when it comes to determining potential signs of inflation.

This is due to the fact that the cost for compensating employees is the greatest cost almost any industry faces, and they tend to be presented in terms of the cost to the company in relation to the amount of profit that is generated when it comes to particular goods and services that are being generated.

Based on its overall outlook, the employee cost index can actually be enough to change the direction of a specific currency completely. This will occur if the actual report comes back in such a way that it is dramatically different from what all estimates expected. This is because these types of compensation costs are almost always passed off onto consumers, which leads to further GDP projection reductions when it is left untreated in the long-term.

This is also one of several indicators that is useful when it comes to determining a country's overall assumed level of productivity. If productivity grows at a slower rate than the rate at which compensation costs are increasing, then the valuation of the related currency is going to decrease and vice versa.

Focus on Interest Rates

After you have a clear idea of the market as a whole and major currencies specifically, you are going to want to focus on what many traders in the futures market focus on the most, the difference in interest rates between various currencies.

This is a crucial step if you hope to form an accurate opinion on the strengths of various relevant central banks, which, in turn, factors into an accurate qualitative analysis of the situation as a whole.

To form a clearer picture in this regard, you are going to want to consider the unemployment statistics of both countries as well as the gap in output that each has. If the economy is increasing, while at the same time, available labor is decreasing, then this will eventually lead to inflation and overall higher rates.

This, in turn, will lead to higher rates from the central bank, which will keep them there until the economy starts heading in the other direction. Keeping an eye on these trends will leave you with a clear idea of what your qualitative analysis has revealed.

Take Stock of Each Country's External Position

When it comes to getting the proper feel for a currency or currency pair, it is important to keep in mind how healthy their balance of payments currently is.

If one of the countries in question has a position that is generally considered to be maintained via asset sales and bank deposits, which can dry up or change direction relatively quickly, then that is less reassuring than a country with long-term commitments such as reserve accumulation or foreign direct investment.

Chapter 8:
The Right Risk and Money Management

Managing Your Money

We cannot stress enough the importance of this part in becoming a successful trader. Anyone's day trading process must have a very strict money management process. First of all, it should be decided how much you are going to risk in your day trading efforts each day, and stick to that amount.

Day trading is in itself a quite painstaking process, and computer-operated algorithmic trades are turning it into a tougher business every day. Most traders who lose big in their trading account do so by day trading or over trading or even irresponsible gambling on short time frames.

It will be beneficial in money management if you know market jargon like bid price, ask price, and how it can impact your trade exit and entry prices. As your experience and expertise grow, you can trade with less loss of money.

Another important step in becoming a successful trader is following the age-old advice of "plan your trade and trade you plan." As these cuts into the chances of having monetary losses, it also increases the chances of maximizing your profits on every trade.

As they say, if you fail to plan, you plan to fail. So, to utilize the maximum potential of trading profits, always first plan your trade and then trade your plan. If you lose confidence in your own capabilities and in your trading plan, especially when you might be holding some market position, then it can result in loss.

One needs to position oneself so as to survive many strings of losses and still be able to maintain a successful day trading method. For this, you must understand how day trading strategies work.

Learning to be a successful trader takes an investment of money and time even if one has the best of tools and trading strategies. Most of the traders mistakenly think that some magic tool or secret will allow them to generate money without any big effort.

Fear, greed, and the egoistical need to prove oneself lead to the road of stock market failure. It would be better to focus on learning which trading strategies and market money management methods work the best for your trading style.

Important Money Management Rules for Traders

Being a trader also means you manage your financial risk and make decisions depending upon your risk-tolerance level.

Follow these great money management rules to safeguard your trading capital and maximize your profits, as well as minimize your losses.

Practice Trade Sizing

Never put more than 10% of your stock trading capital in any single trade. As an example, if you have a trading capital of $25,000, any of your single trades should not utilize more than $2,500.

Keep Strict Stop-Losses

For stocks priced over $10, try putting a mental stop-loss of at least 10%, as well as a hard stop-loss of at least 20%. For stocks priced less than $10, keep stop-loss at 20%.

A mental stop-loss conveys the meaning of keeping a watch at a 10% loss level in your trade. Suppose at the end of the day you check your portfolio and find that one of your stocks is down by more than 10% from its purchase price. Then you have to watch that stock cautiously and check the related corporate news to see if there have been any significant changes that have caused your stock price to drop.

Hard stop-losses, on the other hand, are real stop orders that are placed with the brokerages. These also work as a safety net in case of any surprise moves in the market direction.

Book Profits

It is always a better practice to take partial profits at the 40% level or more. That means, once the trade has earned a 40% profit, then you should book some profit and leave the rest to continue in the trade. By doing this, you can make sure of getting back your initial investment amount as well as some profits.

Trailing Profits

Whenever you have earned greater than a 15% profit, shift your stop-loss towards the break-even point, and go on to complete it until you get out of the position. This is known as "trailing stop." You need to think about initiating such a technique following the initial 15% profit.

Stay Away from Margin Trading

Make use of margin stock trading sensibly, or you may suffer a loss of more than your original investment. Margins are usually an excellent method of growing your primary stock investment. At the same time, if they are not observed carefully and carried out correctly, this kind of stock investing technique can lead to large losses quickly. A well-known trader stated the whole thing as: "Big positions imply bigger problems."

Small and Steady Wins the Race

Do not attempt to become rich quickly. Begin with little capital and develop your self-confidence as well as your trading account gradually but certainly. Consistency will be the name of the winning game. When you have constant trade returns following a lengthy time-period (more than one year), and including surviving lower periods in the market, you could be able to gradually improve your capital exposure.

Diversify

In a case where you have 20 stocks and one of your options crashes suddenly, you suffer a total loss in that stock. It is uncommon but sometimes happens. Then, you would have lost just 5% of your trading capital. Not too horrible. You will survive, and you may go on trading without substantial harm.

On the other hand, if you do not have an effective money management strategy and diversify your trades, putting all your capital in single trades will make your profits continue to take hits, and eventually, you could lose most of your trading capital. You could even get completely wiped out of the markets.

Control Your Risk

If you are a newbie in trading, it is recommended that you begin with a paper trading practice system. Maintain a written record of all your stock trading and record all feelings and errors you go through while trading. After you complete roughly a month, begin a little trading with real cash. Yes, little! Remember: Large positions mean large problems.

Use Limit Orders to get in and get out of a position. Market orders may assure you a fill, but not at the price you wanted. A limit order placed a bit below the last close usually gets fulfilled, most of the time. Simply because a stock generally does a retracement after the initial part of the session.

In case you cannot check the market all through the day—and several of us can not—then the market order would get the job done. Remember that the price you may pay whenever your order is carried out could be a lot higher (or lower) compared to what you anticipated.

The greatest error investors commit when practicing a trading method is to follow it blindly. The method works exactly how it is, but there are always a number of variables that you need to take into consideration.

Keep an Eye on Brokerage

Maybe you do not realize, but this is the biggest money eater when you enter the trading ring. There are hidden charges that eat into your profits or compound your losses. Most of the time, your broker will hide less expensive brokerage schemes and try to sell you some scheme that is beneficial for his business, not yours. So check all brokerage offers carefully. Always check your trading statement to see if you are being charged unnecessarily.

Money Management Skills

Do you know your income expenditure? Do you know your shopping, clothing, and entertainment expenses?

Money Management is a life skill that is not taught in the school curriculum. Most people learn it from our parents how to handle money.

Since most people didn't learn about financial skills in school, you can still learn them now. Here are some of the Money management aids you can follow to improve your skills.

Set a Budget

Track how you spend your money. Do you spend on food, movies, entertainment, and clothes? Do you frequently have an overdraw of your bank account? If this is true, then set a budget. Check your bank statements and note down how much is your expenditure categorically. You will find out how much wastage of money you are not aware of.

Spend Wisely

Have a shopping list when you go to the grocery store? Do you first check the price of an item before putting the item in your basket? Use coupons if available. Use online resources and mobile apps to stay focused on your expenditures.

Monitor your spending! By not being attentive to these small tips, you will keep on losing money. It takes time to get coupons, and It takes some effort to find coupons and writing a shopping list and checking the price of an item before buying. It will all be worth it in the long run.

Balance Your Books

Most people rely on going online to look at their bank balance. By doing this, you won't be able to know how much you are spending at the moment. The best advice is to be accountable by recording all your expenses; you will have avoided overspending.

Set a Plan

You must have a plan for you to accomplish anything. For you to go from location A to B, it won't be possible without a GPS to show the routes. You will end up driving aimlessly going nowhere.

This is similar to not having a financial plan. You will always be broke and not knowing where your money is spent on. "Where did that money go?" With a great plan, you will be able to track your money and expenditures.

Think Like an Investor

The education system does not teach about handling money, mainly how to invest in growing your wealth. The rich people did not just save $500 a month; they learned how to grow their savings and invest. Turning that $500 into $1,000, then into $10,000 and eventually into $100,000 and more.

By investing and growing your money, you will have secured a stable financial future. Think like an investor, and see your money grow.

Have the Same Financial Goals As Your Partner/Spouse

If you're married and you have a joint bank account, then learn to work together. You must both agree with the financial goals.

Make a budget and also see a financial adviser to learn how to invest your money. You must ensure that you have the same financial goals and stay focused.

Save Money

Have a strong commitment to saving your money and securing your future. You can improve your financial situation and make it better! But you need to start with the decision to do so. Make a decision to start saving your money and improving your management skills.

Importance of Money Management

Sticking to a budget and living within your means—is proper money management. Look for great price bargains and avoiding bad deals when purchasing. When you start earning more money, understanding how to invest will become an essential way of reaching your goals, like having a down payment for a home. Understanding the importance of excellent money management will help you achieve your plans and future goals. Some of the importance of Money Management are:

Better Financial Security

Being cautious of your expenditures and saving, you will be able to save enough for the future. Saving will give you financial security to deal with any unexpected expenses or emergencies like loss of employment, your car breaking down, or even saving for a holiday. Having savings, you will not have to use a credit card to settle crises. Saving is a crucial part of money employment as it helps you build your financial security for a secure future.

Take Advantage of Opportunities

You may encounter opportunities to invest in a business to make more money or an exciting experience like a good deal on a holiday vacation. A friend may inform you of a great investment opportunity or get a great once-in-a-lifetime dream holiday vacation. It can be frustrating not having the money to jump right into these opportunities.

Pay Lower Interest Rates

With excellent money management skills, you can determine your credit score. The highest score means you pay your bills on time and with low-level total debt. Having a higher credit score, you can save more of what you have and have a lower interest rate for car loans, mortgages, credit cards, and even car insurance. And there is the chance to brag to your friends about your high credit score at the parties.

Reduce Stress and Conflict

Paying your bills on time can have a relieving feeling. But on the other hand, being late in paying your bills cause stress and have a negative impact like a shutdown in your gas and water supply. Always being broke before your next paycheck can bring conflict and a significant amount of stress for, couple.

And, as we all know, stress brings health problems, experts say, like hypertension, insomnia, and migraines. Being aware of how you can manage your finances so you have extra cash and savings can put your mind at ease. You will enjoy a stress-free life.

Earn More Money

With your income growing, your financial planning will not only include budgeting for monthly expenses but also figuring out where to invest the extra cash that has accumulated.

Knowing different kinds of investments, for example, stocks and mutual funds, you can earn more money from the investments than what you could have made by leaving the money in your savings account in your bank.

But be aware not all investments are recognized as a good investment idea, for example, offshore casinos. One of the best benefits of having investments, you can be at work earning monthly income, and your investments, on the other hand, are making more money for you.

More Saving and Time

Excellent money management can assist in avoiding your finances from spiraling out of control. It is easy to be in debt if you are unaware of how all your income it's spent monthly.

Effective money management means better use of your spare time. You can spend time with your family and friends; by having a clear budget, you will be able to plan for fun days out as you will have available cash to do so.

Peace of Mind

Excellent money management gives you some level of calm and peace of mind. With your income and savings, you can handle any financial demands with the confidence that you have the resources to handle any need that will arise.

Managing Your Money

Investing can seem daunting. You may feel timid when you begin to invest. There are also options to choose thousands of shares and at least that amount of money. And then you still need to determine when it's time to buy and sell. For beginners, the stock market can seem incredibly profitable, dangerous, and confusing. Some basic lessons from the stock market can already save you from the most common mistakes and difficulties. That way, you will stay motivated to learn more about investing.

Start with a Diversified Basis

Leonardo DiCaprio stated in the famed "Wolf of Wall Street" movie: "Simplicity is the ultimate sophistication." A good portfolio excels in a good diversification strategy. A portfolio does not have to contain 30 items, but a correctly balanced mix that keeps risk and returns in balance. Or, as John Templeton said: "Diversify. In stocks and bonds, as in much else, there is safety in numbers." There are plenty of options: from gold, over ETFs, to real estate, currencies, index funds, or shares. Create a clear portfolio where you, as an investor, know how to deal with the risk.

Build in a Buffer for Yourself

Investing is never without risk. The risk-free investment does not pay off; it only costs money. To avoid jeopardizing your healthy financial situation, put some money aside in advance. We usually assume that six months of fixed costs is enough to bridge worse times. If there are indispensable opportunities in the financial markets, you can still use part of this capital to participate. Do estimate whether these opportunities are worth your buffer.

Search for the Adventure and Discover

If there is still some financial breathing room, you can always look for the adventure. A more aggressive investment means more risk but also a potentially higher return. Again, you can limit the danger here by diversifying. As they say about the channel: "Don't put all your eggs in one basket."

Limit Losses and Cash Your Winnings

Every investor experience it sometimes. You have a fantastic share in your portfolio, and week after week, it performs better. And suddenly, there is a turning point, you have hope for recovery, but the decline continues. Until it gets to a phase where you get to make decisions. If you are not prepared to undergo such a rollercoaster, then be wise. Is your investment doubling? Then sell half and secure your investment. When you purchase a share, you can work with a stop-loss order. A percentage of 20% is common.

View the Whole Financial Picture

Making a profit on an investment is quite a pleasant feeling. But investments are not alone, not on an island, or floating in a vacuum. Investments are part of your total financial life. Many asset managers give their clients wise advice: you have to manage your accounting as a business.

Feel Comfortable with Your Investment

Many people who invest and invest today grew up in a different spirit of the times. Thirty years ago, it was fashionable to get as much return as possible. Thanks to the internet, the declining pensions, and changes in the banking landscape, a lot has changed over time. Modern investing and investing are mainly focused on risk and no longer on returns. Most people who invest because of a supplementary pension are focused on avoiding losses instead of making big profits. So, their hope is not to become rich or richer per se, but to have enough capital in their old age to survive.

Investing Is Not a Hobby

Don't get us wrong: investing can be incredibly fun, but you cannot view it as a non-binding hobby. Of course, big banks see investing as a very competitive business. That's why it's best to look at your portfolio through the eyes of a professional. It is important to understand your portfolio well, understand where your profit but also loss comes from. You must also be able to understand the companies in which you invest. Once you have completed this entire process, everything becomes so much easier. "Will this investment or investment earn me money, or will I tear it off?" An obvious question is not always asked.

How to Manage Risk

Risk management will help shield a dealer's record from losing the entirety of their cash. The hazard happens when the dealer endures a misfortune. On the off chance that it tends to be overseen, the dealer can open oneself up to profiting in the market. It is a basic yet regularly ignored essential to effective dynamic exchanging. All things considered, a merchant who has produced significant benefits can lose it all in only a couple of awful exchanges without an appropriate hazard the executive's methodology.

Consider the One-Percent Rule

A great deal of informal investors pursues what's known as the one-percent rule. Fundamentally, this dependable guideline proposes that you should never put over 1% of your capital or your exchanging account into a solitary exchange. If you have $10,000 in your exchanging account, your situation in some random instrument shouldn't be more than $100. This technique is normal for brokers who have records of under $100,000—some even go as high as 2% if they can manage the cost of it. Numerous merchants whose records have higher adjustments may decide to go with a lower rate. That is because as the size of your record increments, so too does the position. The most ideal approach to hold your misfortunes within proper limits is to keep the standard underneath 2%—and you'd hazard a considerable measure of your exchanging account.

Setting Stop-Loss and Take-Profit Points

A stop-misfortune point is a cost at which a broker will sell a stock and write off the exchange. This frequently happens when the exchange doesn't work out how a dealer trusted. The focuses are intended to avert the "it will return" mindset and point of confinement misfortunes before they heighten. For instance, if a stock breaks underneath a key help level, merchants regularly sell as quickly as time permits. For instance, if a stock is moving toward a key opposition level after a huge move upward, dealers might need to sell before the time of union happens.

Instructions to More Effectively Set Stop-Loss Points

The setting of stop-misfortune and take-benefit focuses is frequently done utilizing specialized examination; however, a crucial investigation can likewise assume a key job in timing. For instance, if a broker is holding a stock in front of income as fervor constructs, the person might need to sell before the news hits the market if desires have gotten excessively high, paying little heed to whether the take-benefit cost has been hit. Moving midpoints speak to the most mainstream approach to set these focuses, as they are anything but difficult to compute and broadly followed by the market. Key moving midpoints incorporate the 5-, 9-, 20-, 50-, 100-and 200-day midpoints. These are best set by applying them to a stock's graph and deciding if the stock cost has responded to them in the past as either a help or opposition level. Another incredible method to put stop-misfortune or take-benefit levels is on help or opposition pattern lines. These can be drawn by associating past highs or lows that happened on huge, better than expected volume. Like with moving midpoints, the key is deciding levels at which the value responds to the pattern lines and, obviously, on high volume.

When Setting These Focuses, Here Are Some Key Contemplations

Utilize longer-term moving midpoints for progressively unstable stocks to lessen the opportunity that a good for nothing value swing will trigger a stop-misfortune request to be executed.

Stop misfortunes ought not to be nearer than 1.5-times the present high-to-low range (instability), as it is too liable to even think about getting executed without reason. Modify the stop misfortune as indicated by the market's unpredictability. On the off chance that the stock cost isn't moving excessively, at that point can be fixed. Utilize referred to central occasions, for example, income discharges, as key timespan to be in or out of the exchange as unpredictability and vulnerability can arise.

Calculating Expected Return

Setting stop-misfortune and take-benefit indicators are likewise vital to figure the normal return. The significance of this count can't be exaggerated or exchanged. It also gives them an efficient method to analyze different exchanges and select just the most gainful ones.

This can be determined utilizing the accompanying recipe:

[(Probability of Gain) x (Take Profit % Gain)] + [(Probability of Loss) x (Stop-Loss % Loss)]

The aftereffect of this estimation is a normal return for the dynamic merchant, who will, at that point, measure it against different chances to figure out which stocks to exchange. The likelihood of addition or misfortune can be determined by utilizing authentic breakouts and breakdowns from the help or opposition levels—or for experienced brokers, by making an informed conjecture.

Diversify and Hedge

Ensuring you benefit as much as possible from your exchanging implies never placing your eggs in a single crate. In case you put all your cash in one stock or one instrument, you're setting yourself up for a major misfortune. So, make sure to broaden your ventures—crosswise over both industry areas just as market capitalization and geographic district. In addition to the fact that this helps you deal with your hazard; however, it additionally opens you up to more chances.

You may likewise get yourself when you have to fence your position. Consider a stock position when the outcomes are expected. You may think about taking the contrary situation through choices, which can help ensure your position. When exchanging action dies down, you would then be able to loosen up the fence.

Capital Management

Characterize a thorough capital administration approach and tail it. Keep theoretical capital separate from speculation capital and downplay it of the general portfolio esteem. Also, ensure you are appropriately promoted consistently. If you don't have at any rate, for example, £10,000 that you can focus on a theoretical view, at that point, you will wind up in a default position. Submitting reserve funds, retirement cash, lease cash, youngsters school investment funds, and so on into theoretical capital ought to be viewed as restrictive for any financial specialist or merchant.

Exchanging Limits

To guarantee that you don't lose your theoretical capital, build up, and pursue exchanging limits for any Futures exchange.

For instance, limit your drawback to close to 10% of your capital for sums under £100,000; for sums somewhere in the range of £100,000 and £500,000, this rate ought to be decreased 1% for each extra £100,000 down to 6% for £500,000; for accounts £1,000,000 + 5% or less per exchange ought to be gambled.

Expand Your Portfolio

This is a typical dependable guideline for financial specialists exchanging crosswise over various resource classes; for example—don't place all eggs in a similar container. Enhance your hazard among in any event at least three not legitimately related markets. The more markets your exchanges are broadened over, the less unstable your portfolio will be, decreasing the danger of acquiring in all-out misfortunes.

Influence

Never utilize most extreme influence as it may be important to cover inert assets in your prospects record, money and reciprocals held in different records, and so on. It is constantly a decent rule to keep an enormous enough cushion to cover intraday instability and point of confinement moves. The size of the support will rely upon the specific markets you exchange and your hazard the board methodology.

Making Sure You Can Handle the Stress

And finally, to manage your risk, you need to make sure that you are actually able to handle the stress that comes from day trading. This is a stressful job. You are not able to just place your money on the market and then walk away from it, checking in on occasion. Rather, you need to be watching your stock the whole day. All those little fluctuations up and down can have a big impact on your potential earnings, and this can add a lot of stress to your day.

If you do not have the time to devote to this, at least on the days that you decide to trade, then this is not the right investment option for you. If you have trouble dealing with stress or you already have enough stress in your life, then day trading is not right for you. If you are not good at making decisions at the last minute and you let your emotions take over, then day trading is not for you.

Day trading can be a great investment option for you to work with, but you need to make sure that you are managing your risks and keeping them as small as possible. With the right strategy and risk management plan in place, even when you lose a little bit of money on an occasional bad trade, you will still be able to make a lot of money with day trading.

Make the Trend a Companion

One may have decided to hold a position for an extended time. However, every trader should recognize that no matter the position they take, there is no fighting against the market trends and movements. Accommodate the changes and make sure that the trading strategies reflect the new aspects; this will help one to reduce risk.

Keep Learning

There is always new information coming up in the market every day. As the world changes, so do the economy and the market. A trader should know how the market functions currently, how it evolved, and where it might be heading.

Use Tools and Software Programs

The use of tools and programs can help one select a good choice and avoid risk. However, it is important to note that these systems are man-made; therefore, aren't entirely perfect. It is best to use them as a tool of advice rather than a complete basis of trading decisions.

Use Limited Leverage

Leveraging is very attractive because it gives a trader the opportunity to make bigger profits. However, leverage also increases the chances of losing capital; therefore, one should avoid taking massive leverage. One wrong move with leverage and the entire account is wiped out.

The Three-Step Risk Management Plan

Step 1: The First Step That You Should Take Is to Determine the Absolute Maximum Dollar Risk That You Will Take for the Trade You Are Planning

It is recommended that as a beginner, you should never risk more than 2% of the equity in your account, but you can choose to go up and down from this number based on how much money you have and how much you are willing to risk. You need to have this amount calculated before you even start trading for the day.

Step 2: The Second Step Is to Estimate the Maximum Risk Per Contract That You Will Take, the Strategy Stop-Loss, from Your Entry

We will learn more about how to do this later because you will have a different stop-loss based on the strategy that you choose.

Step 3: Take the Number from Step 1 and the Number You Got from Step 2 so You Can Calculate the Max. Number of Contracts You Can Use

This will give you the maximum number of contracts that you can trade each time. Do not go about this level, or you are increasing your risk too much.

Let's take a look at how this would work. Let's say that you will get some futures contract, and you have $40,000 in your account. If you stick with the rule of only using 2 percent, then you would limit your risk to $800. We will be conservative for this trade as beginners and only risk 1 percent of the account, or $400. Now we have finished step one.

As you are monitoring the futures contract, you decide to sell the short it when it reaches $50, and you want to cover them at $48, with a stop-loss at $51. This means that you will be risking about $1 per contract. Now let's say that the futures contract has a value of 400$ per 1$ move. This will be step 2.

Now we are moving on to step three. We will calculate our size by dividing the numbers in step 1 and step 2, so we can find the maximum size that we can trade. For this example, we would be able to purchase a maximum of 1 contract.

Chapter 9:
The Correct Trading Psychology

Why Trading Psychology Is Important

Most people fail in day trading because they start at the wrong end. They start by learning trading skills first, then move on to money and risk management techniques, and the last stop is to learn, superficially, about trading psychology.

In fact, the right sequence of learning day trading should be learning the trading psychology first, then money and risk management techniques, and the last part should constitute learning the trading skills.

It is very easy to learn technical analysis and how to use technical indicators. But it is very difficult to control one's emotions like fear and greed while trading or astutely manage money while day trading.

If you look at people in different fields, you will find the mindset is the main difference between those who reach the pinnacle of their chosen career and those who remain mediocre. Be it business, science, technology, sports, or any other creative pursuit; people who train their minds for success are the ones who win the race.

In intraday trading also, hundreds and thousands of day traders use the same methods of technical analysis; however, only a few of them succeed in making profitable trade, and others go home with losses. It is the trading psychology that makes the difference between successful traders and those who failed.

Every trader, who tries to learn day trading, knows that there are certain rules to be followed, and still, the majority of them fail to do so find; therefore, if you want to succeed in day trading, you must pay attention to how you react to markets. Stock trading is nothing but watching the price rise and fall and trading off with the trend. But still, traders fail to follow this simple method of trading.

Day trading happens 90% in the mind of a day trader, and only 10% in what happens in markets. A day trader takes decisions based on what he or she thinks is going to happen in stock markets and not on what is happening. This is the biggest mistake day traders make, and the reason is their emotions.

To overcome this psychological hurdle, day traders must learn how to manage their trades without emotions. They can do so only with the help of technology and self-discipline. If they do not have self-control or do not follow a disciplined trading plan, they cannot make profits in stock markets.

At a fundamental level, traders' emotions usually drive markets across the globe.

There are essentially two sentiments and states of mind that determine failure or success in stock trading: greed and fear. A trader's emotional nature largely establishes if he/she is going to be successful in stock trading. In establishing trading success, any trader's trading psychology can be as crucial as some other qualities, like knowledge, skill, and experience. Self-discipline, as well as risk-taking, are two extremely crucial parts of trading psychology. For the success of one's trading plan, following these factors is very important. Although fear and greed are definitely the two common emotions related to trading psychology, some other emotions also generate trading habits, such as hope and regret.

To have an understanding of trading psychology, just think about a few examples of the emotions connected with it.

Greed is usually an extreme wish for riches. Greed frequently motivates traders to remain in a profitable trade more than is sensible, in an attempt to get more profits from that trade, or even undertake big risky positions. Greed can be most evident in the last stage of bull markets, where speculation operates on a wider level, and traders and investors become careless.

On the other hand, fear makes traders exit positions too early or even stay away from tasking risk due to anxiety about big losses. Fear can be prevalent in the times of bear markets, which, as a powerful emotion, can induce traders and investors to do something irrational in their rush to close the trade. Fear usually turns into panic, which usually provokes markets to fall at a considerably faster pace compared to their upward trend.

Regret is another emotion that could cause a trader to enter a trade after originally missing it, as the stock changes too quickly. It is against trading wisdom and quite often leads to the trader entering way too late in the trade.

Successful traders follow some common psychological rules that add to their success. These include:

- They do not over trade. They know their limits.

- They preserve their trading capital through risk management to gain trading success.

- They maintain their trading discipline at all times.

- They know the difference between not going against the trend and following the herd.

Psychologically Approach Toward Success

It may not seem to be a significant factor on the surface. However, psychology plays a huge role in the way investors conduct their trades. Psychology is arguable the most important aspect when investing. The fact of the matter is that for all of the analysis and research that you can conduct, you may find yourself falling victim to some of the most common issues that occur traders. When an investor can control their emotional responses to the way trades are conducted, there is a greater possibility of success.

The most important factor you can put into practice when it comes to devising your investment approach is realistic expectations. This means that you are aware of the fact that investing takes time and effort. Of course, you're not expecting to take years before making a profit. However, you should keep in mind that starting small can ultimately pay off in droves later on. When you start small, you can build momentum. When you build momentum, there is a snowball effect that makes you make more money. Sure, it's tempting to think that you could make a year's salary when in a single trade. Still, then again, you will eventually reach that level after gaining the experience that top traders have gained. It's like pilots; as they accumulate flight hours, they can fly without instrumentation, relying on their experience and better judgment. Now, that doesn't mean that the pilot no longer needs the plane's instrumentation. It just means that they can use their judgment, especially when unexpected circumstances arise.

Also, having realistic expectations is vital to ensure that greed doesn't get the better of you. You see, greed is a very powerful force, particularly when you are good at investing. There is a temptation to take greater and greater risks. Eventually, though, you make one mistake that can derail a long time's worth of success. So, having realistic expectations is a great way of curbing the temptation to take unnecessary risks.

Fear

Fear can be one of the most very dangerous weapons that we use against ourselves. It holds us back from the things we want and makes us push away the things that we need. If you let fear control your life, you'll never really be in charge of any of your thoughts or emotions. Fear can make us nervous, grumpy, and even sick. Almost as bad as this, it can make us lose a ton of money.

Those going into options trading need to make sure that they don't allow fear to hold them back. Though you have to be cautious, you should understand that you can't be too afraid of making a move you might trust. Know the difference between being smart and safe and blinded by worry.

Looking at the Analysis

It's important to understand how to perform a proper technical analysis not just to determine the value of a certain option but also to make sure you don't scare yourself away with any certain number. You might see a dip in a chart, or a price projection lower than you hoped, immediately becoming fearful and avoiding a certain option. Remember not to let yourself get too afraid of all the things you might come across on any given trading chart. You might see scary projections that show a particular stock crashing, or maybe you see that it's projected to decrease by half.

Make sure before you trust a certain trading chart that you understand how it was developed. Someone that wasn't sure what they were doing might have created the display, or there's a chance that it was even dramatized as a method of convincing others not to invest. Always check sources, and if something is particularly concerning or confusing, don't be afraid to run your own analysis as well.

Hearing Rumors

If you are someone that hangs around with other traders, maybe even going to the New York Stock Exchange daily, there's a good chance you are talking stocks with others. Make sure that any "tips" or "predictions" you hear are all taken with a grain of salt. Tricking others into believing a certain thing is true about different stocks and options can sometimes dapple into an area of legal morality, but it's important to make still sure you don't get caught up with some facts or rumors that have been twisted.

You should only base your purchases on solid facts, never just something you heard from your friend's boyfriend's sister's ex-broker. While they might have the legitimate inside scoop, they could also be completely misunderstanding something that they heard. Before you go fearfully selling all your investments from the whisper of a stranger, make sure you do your research and make an educated guess.

Accepting Change

As animals, we humans are constantly looking for a constant. We appreciate the steadiness that comes along with some aspects of life because it's insurance that things will remain the same. Sometimes, we might avoid doing something we know is right just because we are too afraid to get out of our comfort zone. Make sure that you never allow your fear of change hold you back.

Sometimes, you might just have to sell an old stock that has been gradually plummeting. Maybe you have to accept that an option is no longer worth anything, even though it's been your constant for years. Ask yourself if you are afraid of losing the money or just dealing with the fear.

Greed

Greed can be one of the biggest issues that certain traders run into. The reason we're doing this in the first place is for money, and some people think that's greedy enough. While we do need money to feed our family, pay off debt, and just have some cash to live from day-to-day, there are other sources of income than stocks. Still, you get the opportunity to make big money just from the money that you already have. If you are good enough at trading, you can even make it your full-time job. To ensure that you are trading for the right reasons, always ask yourself questions. Why do you need to take such a big risk? Is it worth sacrificing money that could go towards a vacation? Are you making these decisions to feed your family, or are you doing it so that you can go on a self-indulgent shopping spree?

We indeed deserve to have some "me time," and we all should spoil ourselves every once in a while, as we can't depend on other people to always do that for us. However, greed can be a downfall if we're not careful.

Know When to Stop

For you to know when to stop can be the most challenging part of life. It's so hard to say no to another episode when your streaming service starts playing the next one. How are we supposed to say no to another chip when there are so many in the bag? Sometimes, if you see your price rising, you might just want to stay in it as long as you can. In reality, you have to make sure that you know when it's time just to pull out and say no.

If you wait too long, you could end up losing twice as much money as you were expecting to make. This is when the gambling part comes in, and things can get tricky. Make sure you are well-versed in your limits and that you are not putting yourself in a dangerous position if you don't trust your own self-control.

Accept Responsibility

Sometimes, we don't want to have to admit that we're wrong, so we'll end up putting ourselves in a bad position just to try to prove it to someone, even just ourselves, that we were right. For example, maybe you told everyone about this great investment you were going to make, sharing tips and secrets with other trader friends about a price you were expecting to rise.

Then, maybe that price never rises, and you are left with just the same amount that you originally invested. You were wrong, but you are not ready to give up yet. Then, the price starts rapidly dropping, but you are still not ready to admit you are wrong, so you don't sell even though you start losing money. You have to know when just to accept responsibility and admit that you might have been wrong about a certain decision.

Discipline

Having a good knowledge and understanding of different stocks and options is important, but discipline might be the most crucial quality for a trader to have. Not only do you have to avoid fear and greed, but you have to make sure to stay disciplined in every other area. On one level, this means keeping up with stocks and staying organized. You don't want just to check things every few days. Even if you plan on implementing a longer strategy for your returns, you should still keep up with what's happening in the market daily to make sure that nothing is overlooked.

On a different level, you have to stay disciplined with your strategy. Decide where personal rules might bend and how willing you are to go outside your comfort zone. While you have to plan for risk management, you should also plan that things might go well. If the price moves higher than you expected, are you going to hold out, or are you going to stay strict with your strategy?

Stick to Your Plan

If you don't stick to the right plan, you might end up derailing the entire thing. You can remember this element in other areas of your life. You can be a little loose with the plan, but if you go off track too much, what's the point of having it in the first place? If you are too rigid, you could potentially lose out on some great opportunities, but too loose can make everything fall apart.

Prepare for Risk Management

Aside from just knowing when to pull out to avoid being greedy, you also need to make sure that you are doing it so you don't end up losing money. Have plans in place for risk management, and make sure that you stick to these to ensure you won't be losing money in the end.

Determine What Works Best

The most important aspect of a trading mindset is remembering that everyone is different. What works best for you could be someone else's downfall and vice versa. Practice different methods, and if something works for you, don't be afraid to stick to that. Allow variety into your strategies, but be knowledgeable and strict with what you cut out and what you let in. Identify your strengths and weaknesses so that you can continually grow your strategies and always determine how you can improve and how you can cut out unnecessary losses.

Exercise Patience

In the world of investing, patience is the greatest virtue you can exercise. Most folks who venture into the world of investing in financial markets are hopeful they can make a good amount of money quickly. However, like anything in life, it takes time before you can become good at it.

This is why professional investors always preach patience.

If you go to your local bank right now and talk to an investment advisor, they will tell you to be patient, especially if it is going through a rough patch. They will tell you that you can make good returns, but you need to stay in the market long enough to see the results. They may even show you calculations of how your money compounds over time, thus giving you fabulous returns after 10 or 20 years.

Now, you surely don't have 20 years to make money at the moment. Well, it might be a good secondary investment, but certainly not something that you'd be betting on. Nevertheless, being patient is essential to making money in any type of investment.

You are only risking a small portion of your overall investment. This means that you can start small, but due to the power of compounding, you can make a serious amount of money.

This strategy has been successful for plenty of investors. But it takes time and study before you can make this strategy work. You need to keep in mind that rolling over money like this requires you to go on a winning streak. Therefore, you must have the right tools and information before making it big.

Implementing an Organized Approach

Your trading approach needs to be systematic. Otherwise, you'll end up placing trades haphazardly. This will only cause you to make mistakes and lose out on potentially big gains. This is why becoming familiar with technical analysis and fundamental analysis is essential. It's important to note that you need to keep a level head as much as possible. This will enable you to make trades so that you won't waste your time and effort.

But being organized implies so much more. For instance, you need to stick to a proper schedule and adhere to the guidelines we have set up in money management. As you create discipline in your investing, you can give yourself the structure you need to be successful. Otherwise, you'll only find yourself guessing at what might happen.

Another integral part of an organized approach lies in getting to know the patterns of markets. This is important insofar as having a clear understanding of how markets can allow you to make the most of the current economic, political, and social situations.

Consider this situation.

A major oil-producing country has taken a serious hit to their economy as oil prices have plunged on the international market. This means that their currency is set to dive. You could potentially take advantage of that dive by buying up some of the currency at a low price. Then, when it rebounds, you can sell it for a profit. Often, shifts in the marketplace happen very quickly. Such fluctuations can lead you to make pennies on an individual deal. But when you compound them, they can make a significant profit.

This example requires you to be methodical in your study of economics and politics. After all, it's hard to get the full picture without having all of the relevant information at your disposal. Moreover, if you don't pay attention to the way events are unfolding in the world around you, you can miss the boat on significant trading opportunities.

Lastly, an organized trading approach will allow you to keep your emotions in check. Once again, this is a fundamental issue to keep in mind. If you cannot keep your emotions in check, they will eventually get the better of you. And while we have touched on greed and anger, it's also important to learn how to manage fear. When there are negative economic conditions, investors tend to panic. When everyone around you is panicking, it is the time when you can keep your cool and make some serious money. By being able to see opportunities where others are panicking, you can seriously make money. But the only way you can seize an opportunity of this nature is to be systematic and organized in the way you approach investing. Otherwise, you, too, will become prey to the fear and panic of other investors.

Defining Your Trading Edge

Just like any business or company, you need to define what your edge is. This edge could be a keen understanding of a particular region of the world. In such cases, you might have a slight edge since you understand the dynamics of a particular currency. This can help you better understand how you can place a trade taking into account factors that other investors may not necessarily be aware of.

When you go about defining your trading edge, it's all about what makes you a successful investor. As mentioned earlier, it could be that you have specific knowledge about a country or region that provides you with incredible insight into the movements of that currency.

Also, you might have the opportunity to dedicate time to research. In such cases, you can become highly successful as you can put in the hours needed to conduct the research needed to gain a foothold on your investment strategy. This is important to note as not all investors have abundant time at their disposal. You might have a financial brain that can help you figure out the numerical side of investing.

For other investors, their experience is a great boost. This experience may be focused on banking, economics, history, or a genuine interest in financial matters. This can be a great advantage to you as you won't have to spend as much time figuring out how markets work. Of course, you may still need to do some legwork though it won't be nearly as much.

That shouldn't hold you back. If anything, your advantage can be a diligent and careful study of markets. It could be patience or even a level head. Your biggest edge might be that you are willing to risk entering markets when things are rough.

Ultimately, your trading edge will emerge as you begin to study the market and see what it's all about. Many times, you won't define your identity until you have gotten some flight hours under your belt. It could be that you gain a better understanding of Asian markets. Perhaps you feel more comfortable with Latin American currencies. Or, you might decide to specialize in only two or three currency pairs. What you choose to do will be reflected in the way you approach your investments.

For most investors, they try various types of deals early on. Then, as they gain a deeper understanding and knowledge of markets, will gradually specialize in a certain type of currency or currency pairs. Some investors make a living out of a single currency pair.

This could be you. But you need to start somewhere. You can't expect to make lots of money without having to define what your approach will be. It doesn't take a Ph.D. or 20 years of experience in financial markets. It takes a careful understanding of the conditions in the market and how you can make the most of those conditions to your advantage. Often, investors are surprised to find they can understand the dynamics of some markets better than others.

Still, developing that intuitive feel comes when you are willing to keep an open mind. This is one of the best traits to assume. Having an open mind will always keep you receptive to the opportunities that the markets have for you.

View Trading as a Long-term Venture

As with most things in life, trading is a venture that takes time and effort to master and be successful. As simple as this concept sounds, this is not the first thing most new traders keep in mind when they first hear and become excited about this business.

To understand this better, let me lay it out for you.

As you browse through the internet, you come across an ad on social media that reads, "Emerson makes $100 a day day-trading from his home. Find out how." Then you think to yourself, "What if I could make $100 a day from home?" "Perhaps I could quit my job." "I've heard of many people who make money from home. Maybe I should try it."

So, you answer the ad.

Then the landing page contains a video describing a trading system in which you could invest as little as $100 and make twice perhaps thrice the same amount every time it gives you a signal.

Then you find endless testimonials from customers who say that it's working and has even made their lives better. Most of them describe the financial problems that they had before they began using the system, which is now gone. Then you start thinking, "Maybe this thing is real." And the system sells for only $300! You say, "I could afford that. I have my credit card."

As you pull out the card to make the purchase, you start imagining the thousands of dollars you are going to get out of this system. How you will suddenly start going on vacation in a few days. How you could get a new car, perhaps a new house. Or even pay your mortgage in full.

Sounds familiar?

Long story cut short, a month after getting this system, you are nowhere near where this system promised it would put you. As a matter of fact, you are $5,000 in debt and no longer trust ads from the internet anymore.

This has happened to countless people the world over and is probably going on now.

Don't get suckered in by the prospect of quick and easy money. Trading is a business just like any other in which you need to put in a lot of hard work, time, money, hope, the risk, among other things, before you can start enjoying its fruits.

Think of it this way. Could you imagine how many years it takes to stay in school in order to emerge as an undergraduate doctor? In case you didn't know, it takes seven. Majoring in other disciplines in medicine takes even longer.

At the same time, think about the years of sleepless nights that a lawyer spends in school studying, trying to master the discipline so that he or she can emerge as a top lawyer. Think of the years it took a businessman to build up a business empire. Think about the deals that went bad, the stiff competition, lack of money to pay workers, among other business headaches.

Why should it be any easier for you? Why do you think that you should strike 1,000%+ return every year just after spending a few weeks learning how to trade?

The point I am trying to make here is this. Dump the get rich quick mindset as fast as you can. If you do, you will have saved yourself a lot of wasted energy and money.

Trading can end up being one of the most rewarding ventures you can find in this world, but in order to succeed in it, you need to develop a long-term view of it and be willing to put in the hard work that is required.

For instance, you need to study books like this one for as long as is necessary. You need to invest your own money in this business. You need to be willing to delay gratification. You need to take risks. You need to network with other people in the business. You need to fight to stay on top of your game.

In the end, if you work at it, you will attain success in it just like any other professional.

Start Viewing Losses As Part of the Game

If you are one of those people who seems to believe that there is a magical crystal ball, the holy grail, that little truthful piece of information that makes a trader win every time, then you had better change your point of view.

In the trading business, there is no guarantee of succeeding every time. All we are trying to do as traders is beat the odds. We have to accept that losses are going to be part of that process no matter what.

This is one of the reasons why the subject of risk management is so important in this business

It comes down to making more money than you lose.

Winning 100% of the time is statistically impossible. Losses come by even to the best in this business. There is a kind of myth going around that the professionals in Wall Street know something that we don't, something that gives them some kind of inside edge. That is simply wrong.

The best in this business have learned the hard way. They have learned that you cannot eliminate losses in this business. They learned a long time that the only secret is to manage than in a way that makes you win in the long run. That is what they strive to do every day. You must do the same if you want to succeed.

This brings me to another point; you need to adopt a system, a strategy if you will, that you prefer and that you prefer to work with above anything else. Then you test it with a demo to see how well it performs in the long run.

Get a feel of the winners and losers your system gives out. As you do this, you will begin to understand that losers are just a part of this game as is winning and that if you manage them well, then you have little to worry about.

As you do this, you will start developing confidence in your system. One of the worst challenges you will ultimately run into in this business is that of hitting a losing period (also popularly known as a losing streak). This is a period during which your system seems to be performing poorly with every signal that comes out of it.

If you aren't experienced or well versed in the knowledge that at times this happens in trading, then you are likely to throw in the towel. If, however, you took the time to learn about the challenges that occur in this business, you will learn that perhaps if you took a break from trading, then you could go back again later when conditions get better.

So, starting today, realize that losses are trading will always happen and are part of the game. If they are well managed, there is less reason to worry about them. Stick to the 2% rule of money management, and you will be okay. Realize that you could be right even 50% of the time and still make plenty just like the professionals do.

Keep Trading As a Part-time Activity

Another successful trick that can help you turning trading into a successful venture is that of keeping it as a part-time activity.

It is very difficult to trade successfully if you are in a position of trying to make a living out of it. Sure, there are professional traders who trade for a living, but most of them are getting a regular paycheck from the firm that employs them. The proceeds from their trading only get paid in the form of bonuses. This is how Wall Street works for the most part.

Big time professionals in trading are the hedge fund managers and other professional money managers. These people charge professional management fees from the people who invest with them, whether or not their performance is at its peak.

If you look at the big picture, these professionals are not depending on the money they are making from their trading, even if they are earning it. This is perhaps why they are so good at the game.

The reason is simple. The best trading decisions are made when you are in a position where you do not need the money.

When you are constantly under pressure of things such as, "How will I pay my rent this month?" or "How will I pay my daughter's school fees?" you are likely to make some very bad trading decisions. You are more likely to take action, such as trading excessively or placing trades when action is not warranted, all in a desperate attempt to make some money.

So how do you deal with that?

Get a day job. Find something else you can always do on the side that will help keep things in order financially and then trade part-time. As we discussed before, you can use swing trading strategies even if you are currently employed. The analysis only takes a few minutes per day, and this is something most of us can deal with.

You can even decide to trade when you get out of work. Markets such as the Forex market trade 24 hours a day, and this guarantees every person in the world that each person can at least find some time to trade that market. You can use this feature to your advantage.

Getting a day job and trading part-time helps in a number of ways. Firstly, it helps you take care of your bills and other financial responsibilities without putting a strain on your trading.

Secondly, it helps grow your account financially. This is especially true if you intend to use trading as a way of investing in order to grow rich. You can always put aside some money every month, so your account grows, and you can trade more.

Thirdly, it takes away the stress from trading. Let's face it, trading can be very challenging. When you are dealing with losing and making money, then stress can build up very quickly. It gets worse if you are thinking of using the money to maintain a decent living.

When you have something taking care of your financial responsibilities, then you are able to relax. When this happens, then you will be to think clearly. You will be patient enough to wait for the right opportunities to trade. If you make decisions from a position like this, then over time, your account only will soar.

Cultivate a Habit of Discipline

Discipline is another habit that trading as an activity demands a lot. If you aren't disciplined, then you will find it very hard to succeed in this business.

So, what is discipline exactly, and how do you cultivate it?

In simple terms, discipline is simply the ability to stick to a certain set of rules or code of conduct. In other words, it is the ability to exercise self-restraint and deny your indulgent behavior in a given situation.

Lack of discipline is a problem that plagues many traders who fail to get consistent results in the markets. In many instances, it is not the lack of knowledge of what to do that is the problem. It is the failure to implement what you know that is often the enemy. For instance, you are probably aware that you should study instead of going out clubbing because your grades are dependent on it. You are also aware that exercising is good if you want to keep physically fit. Additionally, you may also be fully aware you are supposed to avoid certain types of meals because they are harmful to your health. But somehow, you still keep doing the wrong things. That is the same case when it comes to trading. You are aware that you should have a stop-loss order in place and stick to it. But somehow, you keep moving it around because you believe that the market will always come back. Over time, your loss grows to unmanageable levels. Likewise, you may already be fully aware that you should stick to one trading system that fits you. Yet, for some reason, you keep hunting for the latest system, the Holy Grail. It is clear what is wrong here. Simply knowing what to or what not to do isn't enough. You need a set of actions that you need to take in order to keep your discipline intact. Those actions include:

Plan Every Trade Ahead of Time

You need to plan every trade and trade the plan.

By this, I mean to say that you should sit down and invest time in coming up with a set of rules that you should always follow. Your plan should contain the following;

1) The market setup that you are waiting for.

2) The rules governing the entry price.

3) The rules governing where you should place your stop-loss order.

4) The rules governing where you should place your take profit order.

If your plan contains the parts above, then you are all set.

Make sure that you have written them down. Do not plan things in your mind and imagine that all is well. A plan is better written down instead of in your mind. You also need to vow to always stick to your plan no matter what.

Go over your plan at the beginning of every day and before you place any trade. It will improve your discipline over time.

Keep a Trading Journal

A trading journal is another vital tool to have.

In the same way, a personal journal records the events of your life on a certain day. A trading journal is meant to record the events that took place on a typical trading day.

In it, you record everything that happened right before and after you took the trade. Did you follow the plan that you had? Did you stick to the 2% risk management rule? Did you wait for the right set up to form before you acted? Were you tempted to move your stop-loss order or to close out the trade prematurely?

Record Everything. Then Review It Later

A trading journal helps serve two important purposes. First, it provides a record that you can always revisit and see what you did right at a given point. At the same time, you will be able to know what you did wrong at a certain point and stay away from it in the future. Secondly, it keeps you in check-in that if you remember that you are going to have to record your trading in your journal, you will try your best and avoid deviating from your plan and making a mistake.

It is another tool that helps you develop your discipline.

Keep a Physical Reminder

A physical reminder, in this case, means a simple note that you write down.

In all likelihood, there are those times when for some reason, you simply deviated from your plan and made a huge mistake that cost you dearly. We all have had such times, and it has probably happened to you in the past.

Maybe you overtraded, maybe you raised your stop-loss, maybe you acted prematurely, and maybe you traded a different setup from the one you vowed to stick to, which resulted in a significant loss to your account. Instead of just letting it go, which increases the likelihood of you repeating that mistake, simply write it down and stick it somewhere. You could stick it on the wall of your home office or at your trading desk, somewhere where you will always see it.

Doing so will always keep you aware of your past actions and will likely curb your habit of repeating mistakes in the future. In conclusion, discipline is a must-have for any trader. It doesn't matter how intelligent you think you are right now or how good a track record you have kept in the past. If you do not make an effort of becoming disciplined, then it will only be a matter of time before you learn otherwise. The tools we have looked at will help you figure that out.

Let's now look at the last point in our discussion of trading psychology.

View Trading As a Game and Not a Way of Making Money

Trading in general needs to be an activity that is fun, exciting, and financially rewarding.

Yet, for some reason, we tend to overcomplicate it and take the fun away from it. This is probably one of the reasons why many fail so terribly at it. One solution to this problem is to change your view of the whole activity and begin looking at it as a game of sorts.

When you think of a game, what comes to mind?

Mostly, we associate games with a lot of fun. We also view games as a way to challenge ourselves mentally. In addition to that, we view games as activities we engage in that have no real consequences in the case of failure.

You can apply the same view in trading.

Pretend that trading is simply a game of points. The points are the money that you invest in it. Your goal in this game is to play and accumulate as many points as you can over time. The nature of the game is you are going to lose your points some of the time and also win likewise.

At some point, when you play and accumulate so many points, you can increase the size of your operations. You can even redeem some of the points into your bank account for use in real life, but that isn't the point.

What matters is that you are simply playing a game that you are enjoying and having fun beating the game as it challenges you to get better. And you will keep playing for as long as you possibly can.

Notice how you feel, aren't you now feeling better? If you have traded before, can you now see how it seems to take away almost all the stress out of trading? Can you now see how it can potentially open up an entirely new world for you? What if you chose to live your life as a trader bearing this perspective?

Now, compare it to this. You are trading a $100,000 account, and you were up 20% this month. And you are thinking to yourself, "Wow, I have made so much money I could buy a car with it!" Then, all of a sudden, you hit a losing streak, and you lose 10%. Then you start lamenting, "I just lost money that I could spend on a holiday vacation." Or you start telling yourself, "Oh my God, that money is equal to my two monthly paychecks! How could I have done that?"

Can you see the difference between these two points of view? One allows you to have fun and the other one puts you on an emotional rollercoaster ride. Which one do you think helps you last longer and succeed as a trader?

If you want to enjoy success as a trader, you have to change the traditional view of money that the rest of the world holds. You have to view trading not as a way of making money but simply as a game of points that you are playing and having fun with it.

If you do so, you will enjoy immense success in this business for years to come, all while managing to stay happy and keeping a level head.

Conclusion

Now that you have made it to the end of this book, you hopefully have an understanding of how to get started trading futures, as well as a strategy or two, or three, that you are anxious to try for the first time. Before you go ahead and start giving it your all; however, it is important that you have realistic expectations as to the level of success you should expect in the near future.

Trading successfully demands time, practical knowledge, and market comprehension. Usually, day trading means holding the stock for just the day and exiting the trade by the end of that session. Day trading does not imply trading EVERY day. Day trading is meant for benefiting from price actions in stocks within a single trading session.

Day trade for just days in any week and you might become a sharper trader in real-time than if you trade every day. Day trading can be quite risky, which means you should mainly trade with money which you can afford to lose. Online trading is fast and simple, but generating money through day trading and online investing demands a lot of time and hard work. There are many types of instruments to trade; stocks, bonds, options, forex, etc. Also, there are various methods of trading, such as day trading, swing trading, long positions, short positions, long-term value investing, etc. It all depends on what you choose to trade and in which manner. In case you don't have much time to trade, then you should think of swing trading rather than day trading. Think about every single trade as the largest winner of your trading profession and trade it with that importance.

The next step is to stop reading already and to get ready to get started taking advantage of the benefits that are unique to the futures market. While it may not be exciting, what this means in practical terms is that it is time for you to get down to business and start doing your homework. While you might want to avoid all of that and jump right in, as previously mentioned, all this is likely to do is to nip your options trading career in the bud before it even begins. You will need to start by considering which type of underlying asset you are going to want to pursue if stock market options don't sound that appealing to you.

With this out of the way, you will then need to consider the current state of the market in question and how you can craft a plan to take advantage of those specifics. Remember, haste makes waste, and in this case, waste is going to be all of the money you are throwing away by not taking the time to go through to reach the success that is otherwise almost in reach. Take things slow, and you are far more likely to find the success you seek.

To become a smart trader, you have to avoid entering any trade at market price. Being aware of market jargon, bid price, and ask price is likely to make your trading functions less difficult. And then, when any trader's experience and abilities develop, they are able to trade without taking a loss. These activities can help you plan your trade and develop it so that you increase the profit from each and every single trade.

Therefore, you must always plan your trade, and always trade that plan in order to achieve its optimum possibilities. Losing self-confidence as well as faith in your trading plan, even while holding a market position, usually leads to losses. A person's day trading strategy should have a stringent money management process. One must realize exactly how day trading strategies function.

As you become a more skilled trader, you can start to create particular trading methods, which perform in the best way in any particular market time. A successful trader would need to build trust in his personal capability to evaluate the market and select possible trades. While trading, constantly observe your trades throughout every single minute during the trading session. Equally important is taking a break from trading, which can assist you with noticing patterns, strategies, and the overall market trend with a new, different viewpoint.

It is very important for traders to obtain information regarding the market before they start their trading activity for the day. Appropriate market research is essential for successful trading. It is important for beginners to obtain insight into market conditions and the trading platform before putting a foot in the trading rings.

Do not let your emotions influence your day trading. Usually, emotions turn intense and can be overpowering in trading. For that reason, you should always trade your plan. Changing or modifying your trading plan during any open trade could be disastrous.

Remember, markets are not our friends or foe; we are. Apply these trading money management and emotion-management rules, and you can surely become a successful trader!

Good luck.

www.ingramcontent.com/pod-product-compliance
Lightning Source LLC
Chambersburg PA
CBHW081429220526
45466CB00008B/2318